S

Communication

Begins At **Home**

How To Listen And Talk Effectively

Ruth Lichen Yeh

Outskirts Press, Inc.
Denver, Colorado

The opinions expressed in this manuscript are solely the opinions of the author and do not represent the opinions or thoughts of the publisher. The author represents and warrants that s/he either owns or has the legal right to publish all material in this book.

Successful Communication Begins At Home
How To Listen And Talk Effectively
All Rights Reserved
Copyright © 2007 Ruth Lichen Yeh
V3.0

Cover Image © 2007 JupiterImages Corporation
All Rights Reserved. Used With Permission.

This book may not be reproduced, transmitted, or stored in whole or in part by any means, including graphic, electronic, or mechanical without the express written consent of the publisher except in the case of brief quotations embodied in critical articles and reviews.

Outskirts Press
http://www.outskirtspress.com

ISBN-10: 1-4327-0084-7
ISBN-13: 978-1-4327-0084-3

Outskirts Press and the "OP" logo are trademarks belonging to Outskirts Press, Inc.

Printed in the United States of America

Dedication

To My Husband, Kok-sei

Acknowledgements

I would like to express my appreciation to the many communities and organizations that have given me the opportunities to speak about marriage and family issues. These experiences raised my awareness of the importance of communication. Among the questions most often asked by my audience was, "How can I improve my communication skill?" I thank those audiences for inspiring me.

I also appreciate my clients who have worked collaboratively with me not only to reach therapeutic goals, but who have also provided me with the insight to understand the effectiveness of communication.

Thanks to my family, friends and my colleagues at the Family Enrichment Clinic in Houston. Your support made this book a reality.

Also, my sincere thanks to my writing coach, Mary Beth Averill and my editor, Katherine Mayfield for their professional guidance and personal support.

Table of Contents

Successful Communication Begins at Home
Introduction

Communication is an important life skill for all of us. In the workplace, we confer with co-workers; when we go shopping we negotiate with storekeepers—we communicate with people every day. But *are we communicating effectively?* If we are not, we may not get adequate cooperation from co-workers on the job, or when we're shopping the shopkeeper may not provide the best service to us. We don't see co-workers or shopkeepers all the time, so those kinds of relationships are not as significant as the ones we share with our family members. But our communication skills in those relationships are the same skills we use within our family system, and successful communication within the family is vital to our well being and happiness.

For more than 25 years I have been a therapist, working with individuals and families to resolve their marriage and family problems. Through my experience with hundreds of cases, I have become strongly convinced that effective family communication is one of the most important building blocks of a healthy and happy family, and contributes tremendously to a fulfilling life in later years.

Poor communication creates unbearable pressure in the family, and influences every aspect of our lives. Once I had a client, an adolescent girl named Betty, who after running away from home, stated, "My parents don't understand me. They don't care about me, and I can't stay there." However, according to her parents, "She is our only daughter, and she left us. We are helpless. Now we're even afraid to talk to her, for fear that she might run away again." In this family, both the parents and daughter were suffering from poor family communication skills. Since they were unable to communicate effectively, they could not understand each other's point of view, so the situation got worse with every new attempt to interact, and eventually came to a standstill.

Communication problems within families are not limited to misunderstandings between parents and children. Difficulties can develop in any family relationship—between ourselves and our spouse, partner, our parents, in-laws or other relatives. The skills that are needed for effective communication vary depending on the relationship. For instance, when talking to our children, we have to consider their ages: talking to a toddler requires different skills than talking to an adolescent. We often find communication problems between different generations as well. With these considerations in mind, this book is divided into the following six parts:

1. Key concepts in effective communication

2. Communicating effectively with younger children

3. Communicating effectively with school-age children

4. Communicating effectively with adolescents

5. Communicating effectively with your spouse and partner

6. All in the family, including parents, in-laws and other relatives.

The issues of blended families are discussed under all in the family, in chapter 6.

Successful Communication Begins at Home is designed to help individuals and families understand the important elements of communication and improve their communication skills. Our homes provide many types of learning experiences, including listening and talking to each other. In fact, most children *listen and say* their very *first word in the family.* Their parents and other family members have taught them to reach that very *first step of communication.* Children learn to communicate by *watching and listening as their families talk.* Home is the place we learn how to listen and talk, and if we learn how to listen and talk effectively and successfully, home is a happy place to live and share. We learn how to interact with others based on what we learn at home, and if we have not learned good communication skills at home, we will have difficulty interacting with others in the world.

Effective communication is not only essential for interpersonal relationships, but it is also essential to work relationships and international relationships. Facilitating an understanding of effective communication between two parties or two countries may help promote a favorable relationship and peace in the world. Nevertheless, effective communication *begins at home.*

The key concepts of effective communication are presented in the first chapter. It's necessary to understand the key concepts in order to make the best use of the information in the following chapters. Skills for communicating effectively with family members at different life stages will be presented in Chapters 2 through 5. Chapter 6 combines communication between different members of the family, an important skill in this day and age when the blended family (due to divorce or death and subsequent remarriage) is very common.

Every chapter has examples or cases presented to facilitate your thoughts and enhance your understanding. Names and identifying information for case examples have been changed for confidentiality. Some cases are composites, incorporating incidents from several families I have worked with.

The purpose of this book is to help readers understand that we learn our communication skills within the family system, and that all members of the family—including ourselves—contribute to that learning process. I hope this book will be a resource for your learning process. To facilitate this process, I have created *a pre-test and a post-test* for you to take, to help you become aware of how accurately you understand "effective communication." I recommend that you take the pre-test before reading this book and take the post-test after you finish reading it.

Learning to communicate more effectively is a valuable life skill. I hope that this book will help you to develop your communication skills, and thus provide you with a richer life experience and deeper, stronger relationships throughout your life.

PRE-TEST

1. You would like to improve your communication. Which areas do you think you need to improve?

   A. ___Talking, expressing.

   B. ___Listening.

   C. ___Both.

2. You are talking to your brother and you have a feeling that he is not listening to you, because he:

   A. _____

   B. _____

3. For the above situation, as an older sibling you feel like changing or correcting him. Which is/are your choice(s)?

   A. ___Confront him, and tell him to pay attention.

   B. ___Change the subject.

   C. ___Try to understand why your brother is not interested in talking.

   D. ___Just stop talking to him.

4. Mr. Stone is a powerful boss. His workers avoid talking to him because he acts in a condescending way towards his subordinates and that makes people uncomfortable.

Mr. Stone's communication pattern is called the:

A. ___Parental ego state

B. ___Adult ego state

C. ___Child ego state

5. If you were working for Mr. Stone, which ego state would you prefer him to use in communicating with you? Explain why.

A. ___Parental ego state

B. ___Adult ego state

C. ___Child ego state

Because:_____

6. A counselor suggested to the mother of an adolescent that the mother use "I" messages to communicate with her son, because they are more effective and more likely to motivate her son. The counselor's suggestion is based on:

A. ___The "I" message secures the mother's position as a "mother".

B. ___The "I" message shares the mother's feelings and is less demanding or criticizing.

7. To teach your child to be an effective communicator, at which stage would you start?

    A. ___You would start when the child is an infant, because communication is sharing and connection.

    B. ___You would wait until the child starts school, because school-age children are more effective in learning.

    C. ___You focus on teaching communication when the child reaches adolescence, because adolescence is a crucial stage.

8. You have a three-year-old son and you are a busy parent. You have to prioritize your time. Which would you choose?

    A. ___You want to spend your time to teach him numbers and help him remember his "ABCs" instead of just playing with him.

    B. ___You play what he wants to play with him, because that shows you are accepting him and helping him establish confidence and autonomy.

C. ___You can be creative in including the numbers or alphabet in the playtime, and keep his interest while playing with him.

9. Your friends have different opinions regarding communication with school-age children. Which one is your belief? Explain why.

A. ___Children should be encouraged to express their feelings and thoughts at any time.

B. ___Training children to refrain from expressing their feelings helps them be patient and endure pain.

C. ___Parents should allow and encourage children to express themselves when the situation is appropriate.

10. Adolescence is a difficult stage for both parents and children. Some effective ways to communicate with an adolescent are to:

A. ___Avoid conflict by ignoring him/her.

B. ___Use "I" messages to communicate.

C. ___Use "you" messages to communicate.

D. ___ Listen with an open minded-attitude.

E. ___ Model respect and trust in your communication.

11. Billy is 17 years old. He is making a decision about college applications. His parents want him to go to the same university as his sister, so his sister can take care of him. Billy tells his parents that he wants to be independent, and that his sister is too controlling. Which suggestion would you give to Billy's mother?

A. ___ Parents have the right to make decisions for their children, so they should insist that Billy apply to his sister's school.

B. ___ Tell Billy that if he goes to the same school, they will buy a new car for him.

C. ___ Tell Billy that college is for study, not "to be independent."

D. ___ Billy's parents need to talk with Billy and understand his feelings and thoughts about going to college.

12. Ted, a 13-year-old boy, returned from his friend Donny's

house, and told his mother, "See, Mom, Donny's mom allows Donny (who is the same age as Ted) to have girlfriends." If Ted's mother asks your advice, which suggestion(s) would you give to her?

    A. Ignore Ted. All adolescent boys are interested in girls.

    B. ___ Don't let Ted associate with Donny because Donny is a bad influence.

    C. ___ Be patient with adolescents, and have an open-minded discussion with Ted.

13. Jan, a high school senior, was having dinner with her parents. Jan's mother started to talk about her friend's daughter, Mary. She said, "You know Mary is going to hold a graduation recital soon, and her mother told me Mary has received a music scholarship. They are lucky!" Jan was quiet, but soon she picked up her plate and left. She went to her room and closed the door. Why did Jan leave the dinner table?

    A. ___ Because of Jan's poor social skills.

    B. ___ Because Mary's success made Jan look bad.

C. ___Because of her mother's negative comparison.

14. Which of the following would be your suggestion to Jan's mother?

    A. ___Knock on Jan's door and apologize to her, and try to comfort her.

    B. ___Knock on Jan's door and tell her that her attitude at dinner was not acceptable.

    C. ___Tell Jan's father to go talk to Jan.

    D. ___Just ignore her—tomorrow is another day for her.

15. A man tells his therapist that he has loved his wife since the first time he saw her. Now he is wondering, "Why is my wife unhappy with me?" He says, "My therapist has told me, 'you both need to improve your communication.' I don't understand!" What is your opinion about this husband's comment?

    A. ___The husband still loves his wife, but his wife may need to share her feelings and thoughts more often. Couple's communication should go both ways.

B. ___The wife may not have felt her husband's love, so he should put more effort into expressing his love.

16. Cultural differences between a couple can provide wonderful learning experiences, yet may create chaotic misunderstandings for the couple. What is your suggestion?

A. ___One partner or spouse needs to be submissive and follow the other partner.

B. ___The couple needs to have an open-minded attitude and be willing to listen and share.

C. ___The couple may ignore cultural differences, because the love between them is more important.

17. Effective communication builds trust in the relationship. Which of the following is helpful in building trust in the relationship?

A. ___Proper self-disclosure.

B. ___Listening but not talking.

C. ___Sweet talk.

18. Conflict is an inevitable issue in human relationships. From the following, which one is your recommendation for resolving conflict?

    A. ___ For the sake of peace, just apologize!

    B. ___ Fight for your own rights. Don't just give in.

    C. ___ Bring out the conflict issue, listen to each other's point(s) and be fair to each other.

19. Mrs. Brown is visiting her adult son, Marc, who is married and has a 4-year-old boy, Jimmy. At 8 o'clock, Jimmy was supposed to take a bath and go to bed, but Jimmy would not follow his mother's instructions. He wanted to continue playing with the new toy that his grandma bought him. Jimmy's mother, Beth, was very upset and loudly yelled at Jimmy. Jimmy cried, and everybody was in a bad mood. Then Grandma stepped in to rescue Jimmy and said, "It's all right. He may skip his bath today. He did not sweat, and he was a good boy today." What would you think about Mrs. Brown's comment?

    A. ___ It creates a "triangulation."

    B. ___ It provides a peaceful instruction.

C. ___Grandma was a helpful rescuer to her grandson.

20. In the above situation, Marc (Mrs. Brown's son) appeared to be uneasy. What is your suggestion for Marc?

A. ___He should talk to his mother nicely: "Mom, the 8 o'clock bath is both Beth's and my decision, and it's a routine Jimmy needs to follow." Then he should help Jimmy take his bath.

B. ___He should avoid involvement by withdrawing to his study.

C. ___He should show support to his wife by punishing Jimmy with a 5-minute time-out.

D. ___He should tell his mother, "Mom, don't spoil your grandkid!"

21. While her daughter was out, Mrs. Block took a telephone message for her, but she purposely did not give the message to her daughter, because she did not like the caller, a friend her daughter was associating with.

A. ___Mrs. Block did the right thing, because she believes that friend is a bad influence.

B. ___Mrs. Block should not withhold the message, but she can discuss her concerns with her daughter at an appropriate time.

C. ___Mrs. Block should just give the message to her daughter regardless of her own concern.

22. Children in blended families need to adjust to their new parents and siblings. The parents need to be able to communicate effectively. Which of the following do you think would be your choice(s)?

A. ___Minimizing communication in order to avoid conflict.

B. ___Communicating with direct and clear messages in order to avoid entanglement.

C. ___Being open-minded and embodying positive attitudes to help the children's communication.

23. Last Christmas was the first holiday together for Lori and Stan. They decided to invite the relatives who live nearby to join their Christmas dinner. After dinner, the conversations were centered on current information about relatives. One of the cousins was in trouble with

substance abuse and had been sentenced to jail. Lori was relatively new in the family and she felt that their discussion was just gossip. What is your suggestion for Lori?

A. ___Just get away from the discussion.

B. ___Since Lori is the hostess; she should initiate a new situation, like suggesting they play a game, or dance.

C. ___Condemn their behavior and stop them from gossiping.

24. The communication in a blended family is not always easy because family members have different experiences and different communication patterns. When June and Ben remarry, they both will have children from previous marriages. From the following list, what would you suggest to June and Ben, so they may have a happy blended family?

A. ___June and Ben need to take time to know each other better, and to take time preparing their children for their remarriage.

B. ___June and Ben need to be open-minded, able to listen and able to express their own feelings and thoughts.

C. ___They should avoid taking sides with their own children in order to be fair to all the children.

D. ___They should set rules that all the members can follow.

E. ___They should support open communication.

F. ___All the above.

The answers to the test follow the Post-test at the end of the book.

Chapter 1
Key Concepts in Successful Communication

The following key concepts will help you understand your own communication patterns and improve your communication skills. We are often unaware of our own communication patterns, so we repeat the same problems again and again, unable to effectively express our needs or feelings.

- Communication starts from your inner self.

- Repetitive patterns in communication.

- Communication is a tool for connection.

- Communication indicates (specifies?) relationship.

- Successful communication is sincere and honest.

- A successful communicator seeks to understand his/her audience.

- Active Listening makes an effective listener.

- Understanding nonverbal communication is essential.

- Understanding the ego state is essential.

COMMUNICATION STARTS FROM YOUR INNER SELF

When you are communicating, you are expressing your inner thoughts and feelings to others and you are revealing your inner self. However, some individuals are *not able to reveal their inner thoughts and feelings* due to a particular environment or the situation. The followings are some possible causes:

1. *Their cultural* or *family system* causes the individual to suppress certain thoughts or feelings and prevents the individual from expressing them.

2. *Some negative or adverse experiences* have caused the individual to become fearful in expressing his/her inner

self to others, and thus that person *avoids the repeating hurtful experiences.*

3. Some individuals may *lack the ability to express* inner thoughts and feelings because they didn't have *proper models and guidance* during their *formative years.*

We learn to listen and to talk from our families, and proper modeling and guidance are important in developing ways to express ourselves. The following case is an example of a person who has been affected by the three situations above.

Example: When I met Sue, she was a lovely 25-year-old woman who had been married for two years. Her husband suggested that she seek professional help for two reasons. She often stayed awake at night crying, and she was plagued by nightmares. Her husband was puzzled and confused because she didn't know how to express or share her feelings with him.

In the session, when I asked Sue about her childhood,

she told me that she had been an unwanted child of an unplanned pregnancy. Because her Christian grandmother had opposed her mother's plans to have an abortion, Sue's mother finally agreed to raise her but she treated Sue badly compared to her other children. Sue was often humiliated and criticized. Her mother would punish her when she expressed her feelings or made comments. Because of this, Sue grew up thinking that speaking up for herself would result in the listener becoming angry with her. In addition, her mother's repeated abuses made it hard for Sue to understand or respond to love with affection. The patterns of *withdrawing and being quiet*, which she had developed in order to cope with her childhood trauma remained with her when she married. Her traumatic experience got in the way of open communication with her husband. *Sue never learned how to express her feelings*. During individual therapy sessions

I established rapport with her by my sincere attention in listening to her childhood encounters and expressing my concern. My model of open communication helped her relax and open up to me. I helped her identify *how she suppressed her feelings*, and encouraged her to speak out about her feelings and her needs. I was a safe person with whom she would share her feelings of sadness, fear and disappointment. When she burst into tears, I supported her in releasing her emotions. As she began to recover from her childhood trauma, she started to get in touch with her feeling of love toward her husband. I supported her in *experiencing that loving feeling and encouraged her to verbalize it* in her own words, a newly learned communication skill. As Sue improved her own communication skills, the couple's communication also improved. As Sue became more able to reciprocate her husband's love and care, she became happier.

The key point of Sue's story is to illustrate that in a *family system, negative experiences in childhood can result in the lack of ability to express the inner self.* Sue relearned a new way of communication which allowed her to become aware of her inner self, and express her feelings and needs. When you have communication problems in your relationships, they may be caused by an inability to express yourself or your partner's difficulty in expressing himself or herself. However, as we see in Sue's case, learning a new communication skill can result in a deeper connection to the inner self and a stronger ability to give and receive love. She became able to express love and receive love from her husband.

REPETITIVE PATTERNS IN COMMUNICATION

There are repetitive patterns in people's communication which are formed through learning. Like all learned behavior, *communication patterns can be relearned (changed)* if the pattern previously learned was not effective. We generally accept that culture, environment and family system shape an individual's communication patterns, because we develop the pattern as children from the home in which we grew up. We often recognize that our family members speak the same way, even using the same words. I am familiar with Asian culture from my own background, and many studies have shown that the Asian parents encourage their children to be *quiet listeners* rather than *talkers.* They discourage their children from making comments or expressing their feelings, because Asian culture respects individuals who are able to suppress personal feeling. Thus, open communication is not encouraged in a traditional Asian family. In Asian communication patterns, whatever happens in the family should stay within the family and never be revealed to any outsiders, because this would result in disgrace and shame being placed upon the family.

Example: Here is a true experience of an Asian-American family. Tom, a kindergartner, told his mother that he wanted to bring family pictures to school for a "show and tell" presentation the next day. According to the child, his friends brought in all kinds of stuff from home for show and tell. His mother disagreed with Tom's idea, as she felt embarrassed that her son was going to talk about their family to other people. This idea of her son talking to the whole class about his family seemed a strange idea to the mother. However, this mother, who had an advanced degree from an American university, reluctantly went along with her son's plea, and let him take the family pictures to school. The kindergartner returned home from school with a big smile on his face. He proudly reported to his mother that his teacher had liked his show and tell, told him that he had given an excellent presentation, and praised his family. Tom was very happy and felt good about himself.

This Asian-American mother learned something from her son: in addition to the traditional Asian family communication pattern of *"remain quiet and listen and don't talk about the family to an outsider,"* the mother learned "show and tell," a new pattern, which allows children to express ideas and share information with others.

People learn different patterns, depending on where they grow up. A friend of mine from Mexico told me that when her family gets together; everyone is very affectionate and openly expresses their feelings. They talk loudly and with a lot of hand motions. She realized that she does not interact with people in that manner here in the States, but when she returns to her hometown she enjoys and participates in the way her family communicates. It's helpful that my friend is aware of her own communication patterns. Thus she can communicate happily and effectively in her hometown as well as in the U.S. Are you aware of your own communication patterns? It is interesting and helpful to pay attention to your communication patterns — if you do, you will create a richer life experience and more fulfilling relationships for yourself.

COMMUNICATION IS A TOOL FOR CONNECTION.

Not only do we express our feelings and thoughts to others, but we also listen to others as well. Verbal interaction is where most of us start the connection that can *bring comfort* to ourselves and others, and enable us to heal other people's hurts. On the other hand, ineffective communication may hurt others; it may also bring people disappointment, frustration and anger. *When we cannot adequately express our feelings we may become depressed.* Depression is a mental health problem of national concern. As a therapist participant in the Annual Depression Screening in Houston, Texas, I have found that many depressed people *have two problems in common.* One is *poor communication skills* and the other is lack of adequate *coping skills.* Both of these problems may result in poor relationships. These two problems make depressed people feel that nobody understands them and that life is meaningless. The sad part is that both problems are caused by their lack of communication skills.

When I treat depressed clients, *I initiate the connection* with them. I begin by listening sincerely to their pain and suffering, and I rephrase what I have heard, then I ask more questions in order to provide opportunities for them to talk more. *By listening* and *asking questions I make a connection* with them. I am modeling good communication skills. I usually see a gradually relaxed mood on their faces. The information I gather from them is a resource that I can use in helping them with their problems. These skills of listening, rephrasing, and asking questions are all skills that you can use with friends or relatives who are depressed. It takes patience, but give it a try. Here is an example of a person I helped.

Example: Kent, a 39-year-old biochemist, was severely depressed, and even attempted suicide after his wife asked for a divorce. He was placed in a hospital. Kent was a hard worker and his employer valued his research, but he hardly ever talked to or interacted with others. He worked late most of the time and seldom spent time with his family. He was not aware of his wife's unhappiness until the day she brought up the issue of divorce. Kent did not have any solution for this, and had no one to talk with about his problem. He felt helpless, and thought life was meaningless, so he wanted to end his life quietly at his laboratory. Fortunately, a co-worker came in unexpectedly and called for help. Kent had been known as a very quiet, diligent scientist. His contribution to the field had been recognized and respected, but he had never expressed his feelings. His wife also respected his professional achievements, but she felt that *they were not connected* as a married couple because he had hardly shared his feelings or asked about her feelings. She was lonely, and felt her husband hardly had time to talk or listen to her. Kent was an absent husband; they were not connected. The problem occurred not only in his family — he was also not connected to others, only to his work.

This time he almost lost his life and marriage. From these painful experiences he realized the importance of communicating and socializing with others. He participated in therapy; his attitude changed, and when he learned to *identify his feelings and express those feelings verbally,* he became more open and connected with others. Kent and his wife practiced how to listen and express their feelings to each other during their couple's therapy sessions. His wife described how lonely she was after she put their baby to bed and waited for him to come home. Kent listened to his wife's statements and feelings attentively; he was touched, and apologized for his ignorance. Kent also expressed to his wife that when she asked for a divorce he felt his whole world become dark, and he could not find a reason to live. Kent and his wife shared their emotions openly, and in doing so they both recognized they *were not connected* before because of *a lack of effective communication.* Kent put effort into *relearning how to listen and how to talk with people.*

Kent learned the hard way; nevertheless he has become a better communicator and is improving his social skills. His family and his colleagues all appreciate this change.

COMMUNICATION INDICATES (SPECIFIES?) THE RELATIONSHIP OF THE COMMUNICATORS

In a family, the pattern of parent/child communication differs from husband/wife communication, because the participants are in different relationships. *Effective communicators are aware of their own (inner) thoughts and feelings* and are *able to express them effectively* to other family members, according to the relationship. As I have mentioned before, I have found that each family has its own unique communication pattern. Some families believe it is *not necessary* to express feelings within the family because they are related and share some degree of intimacy. For instance, they believe it is not necessary to say, "thank you" or "please" or "I am sorry" to their own family members, even if they have these feelings inside. My experience as a therapist suggests that many unhappy marriages are unhappy because the couples do not share their feelings. I believe that it is important for *a married couple to share feelings with each other throughout all stages of marriage.* Couples often acknowledge that they used to talk and share and appreciate each other more in the early stages of their marriages, and said they were even better during the premarital stage. However, they gradually began to neglect each other year by year, not sharing feelings as they had before.

Successful communication promotes happy relationships in the family: *the messages of care and*

Love are received and delivered, and trust and confidence within the family are secured by successful communication in the family

SUCCESSFUL COMMUNICATION IS SINCERE AND HONEST

The purpose of communication is to express *the truth. It is important to be accurate and to refrain from exaggeration*. People sometimes have a tendency to exaggerate during the conversation. Some examples: "He is *too* lazy, and doesn't do anything but watch TV," or "She is *never* on time." Such exaggerations are often spoken without the speaker's realization. Nevertheless, they are *not truth but exaggeration*, and they may create a negative impact on interpersonal relationships. The communication is much more effective if the message is true and the feeling is sincere. For the same conversation, you might use these words: "He likes to watch TV and doesn't have enough time for doing yard work," or "She is often late for work because her bus doesn't stay on schedule." It *states the fact, not an exaggeration,* and shows the speaker's *sincere attitude.*

A SUCCESSFUL COMMUNICATOR KNOWS HIS/HER AUDIENCE

A successful communicator needs to understand the listener's background and areas of interest. According to psychologist Erik Erikson, we learn different tasks at different life stages to meet our developmental needs. He divides those tasks and needs into eight stages, which he calls psychosocial development stages, moving from infancy through late adulthood. Understanding the tasks and needs of each stage is necessary for improving communication. As successful communicators, we need to understand *the listener's background and interests, and recognize how those are closely related to the individual's developmental stage.*

The following is an outline of Erikson's psychological development stages: (adapted from Erikson's 1959 Identity and the Life Cycle)

The Involvements:

* Physiological Change
* Biological Demands
* Confronted with Societal Constraints
* Ratio of "Satisfactions" to "Denials"
* Socializing Partner
* Family History

Stages of Psychosocial Development:

Stage I

Age: 0 to 1, infant
Psychosocial task: trust vs. mistrust
Significant relations: parent(s), care taker
Psychosocial virtues: hope, faith
Mal-adaptations: sensory distortion – withdrawal

Stage II

Age: 2 to 3, toddler
Psychosocial task: autonomy vs. shame and doubt
Significant relations: parents(s), care taker
Psychosocial virtues: will, determination
Mal-adaptations: impulsivity – compulsion

Stage III

Age: 3 to 5, preschooler
Psychosocial task: initiative vs. guilt
Significant relations: family
Psychosocial Virtues: purpose, courage
Mal-adaptations: ruthlessness – inhibition

Stage IV

Age: 7 to 12, school age
Psychosocial task: industry vs. inferiority
Significant relations: schools and community
Psychosocial virtues: competence, cooperation
Mal-adaptations: inertia

Stage V

Age: 12 to 18, adolescence
Psychosocial task: ego-identity vs. role-confusion
Significant relations: peer groups, role models
Psychosocial virtues: fidelity, loyalty
Mal-adaptations: fanaticism, repudiation

Stage VI

Age: 20's, young adult
Psychosocial task: intimacy vs. isolation
Significant relations: partners, friends
Psychosocial virtues: love
Mal-adaptations: promiscuity – exclusivity

Stage VII

Age: late 20 to 50's, middle-age adult
Psychosocial task: generativity vs. self-absorption
Significant relations: household, workmates
Psychosocial virtues: care
Mal-adaptations: overextension – rejectivity

Stage VIII

Age: 50's and beyond, older adult
Psychosocial task: integrity vs. despair
Significant relations: mankind or "my kind"
Psychosocial virtues: wisdom
Mal-adaptations: presumption -- despair

Referring to the above psychosocial stages will help us to choose the *level or kind of language* we use to communicate effectively. For example, talking to a three-year-old is different from talking to a 30-year-old mother. A three-year-old child would prefer to listen to a story-like form of talking in simple language; by contrast, a 30-year-old mother would enjoy talking a topic, such as her child-rearing experience or other common interests. The *choice of time and place* for communication also needs consideration. Here is a typical ineffective communication between a parent and her adolescent son.

Example: Maria's son, Ben, is a high-school student who does not want to engage in conversation with his mother, because he knows the *topic of conversation* is not of interest to him; it's an old subject (reminding him again about college applications), and the *time and place are not convenient* for him. Her son is about to go out with friend — he is not interested in listening to his mother repeat herself. Both Maria and her son are unhappy, *because of ineffective communication.*

The above example shows that Maria was not aware of her teenage son's need and interests. He is an *adolescent, he is at an identity formation stage,* struggling to make decisions and learning to become independent.

Parents like Maria are often *preoccupied by parental duties*, and overlook the children's developmental tasks and their needs, so they can lose the ability to communicate effectively with their children, and may even disrupt the parent/child relations. To improve our communication, we need to understand our listeners, and be aware of their interests and needs according to their stage of life. Erickson's model of psychosocial development stages provides helpful knowledge.

ACTIVE LISTENING MAKES AN EFFECTIVE LISTENER.

If we want to be successful in communicating, we have to listen actively. Although we learned to listen before we could talk, many of us are not active listeners. Active listeners are involved in and participate in the communication. They *provide feedback, asking questions* or even responding by nodding their heads quietly. Feedback indicates that you are listening. In addition, asking questions indicate that you are interested in what the speaker is saying and that you are involved. Effective communication involves *two parties*—one who talks and the other who listens. Without an active listener, the speaker can become frustrated, and may wonder if the other person is not listening or does not care. On the other hand, if the speaker talks continuously and the listener has no chance to respond or ask questions, the listener can be also frustrated and become an inactive listener.

Example: On Sunday morning, Ron was reading the newspaper while his wife was talking to him about their plans for the day. He kept reading without acknowledging her, and his wife became upset, complaining that he was not listening and did not care about her. Ron argued that he was listening. Most likely, Ron *heard* his wife talking *but he was not actively involved*, because he was not an active listener. *If you are an active listener, people like to talk to you, and you are a likable person because you are sincere and interested in people.* Active listening is a valuable interpersonal skill, and includes proficiency in the next area to be discussed.

UNDERSTANDING NONVERBAL COMMUNICATION

We learn to listen from our family when we are children, and most of that is listening to verbal communication. However, an understanding of nonverbal communication is essential for effective communication. *Nonverbal messages reveal the speaker's feelings and convey attitudes.* As an active listener, you are decoding those *nonverbal cues,* such as *gesture, posture, facial expressions, eye contact,* etc. The following are common nonverbal messages that we often encounter in our daily lives. Observing these nonverbal messages understanding the meaning behind the unspoken words will help you communicate more effectively.

1. Gesture and posture—body movement: The communicator's posture—leaning forward or backward or slumping downward—are indications of their level of interest in conversation and show the feelings of the listener. A 9-year-old boy, Denny, described to me how his soccer team had won last week's game. He was happy to share his winning experience with me, and he moved closer to me and bent forward and moved his hands to explain the details of the game. His mother came in shortly thereafter, and when she started to complain about how poor his math work was, Denny slumped further and further, and sank into the armchair. Obviously, the change in Denny's posture spoke for his feelings.

The most popular gesture is known as "talking with your hands." Just as with verbal communication, where people who come from the same family talk the same way and use the same words, in nonverbal communication people from the same family will move their arms and hands the same way when they talk. It is absolutely true that we learn to listen and talk from our family, whether verbally or nonverbally. Successful communication begins at home, where we learn to listen and talk both verbally and nonverbally.

2. Facial expression: Among the forms of nonverbal communication, facial expression is probably easiest to understand. For instance, a smile expresses a happy feeling; a wrinkled forehead indicates the person is stressed or frustrated; and raised eyebrows can communicate anger or surprise. *Eye contact* is another facial expression that is part of effective communication, because eye contact can be a significant indicator of the communicator's attitude. *We usually associate good eye contact with positive implications..* Eye contact indicates that you are actively engaging in conversation and that you are sincere, and it shows your confidence in communicating. For instance, if you were at an interview, you would look at the interviewer directly and listen attentively in order to understand the information and show your interest in the interview. In the same way, you read your interviewer's intentions by observing the person's facial expression and his eye contact with you. Lack of eye contact may suggest disinterest or discomfort. However, it should be noted that there are *cultural differences in the implication of eye contact.* Some cultures avoid eye contact when listening to an elder or to an authority, because direct eye contact implies lack of respect to the speaker. Therefore, when a younger person listens to the elderly he/she needs to purposely look down to indicate respect to the elder in those cultures even if the young person is actively listening.

3. Tone of voice or other vocal nuances are also worth mentioning. When two parties are talking, their voices may infuse the "words" with shades of deeper meaning. In many cases, *tone, pitch* or *volume of voices indicates the emotion of the speaker.* An active listener needs to pay attention to these vocal nuances. Vocal qualities may express feeling of anger, frustration, sadness, or even happiness or excitement, sometimes without any other corresponding nonverbal cues. Have you noticed these examples in your daily life? It's helpful to pay attention to these nonverbal cues. One way to improve your active listening skill is to become aware of the nonverbal messages people communicate.

The following suggestions can help you practice active listening:

Feedback: Giving feedback is a sign of active listening. Feedback consists of processing what you hear and relaying it back to the speaker. Feedback clarifies that we understand what is said and what the speaker intends. Feedback may also play a supportive role for the speaker in term of reinforcing the speaker's message.

Paraphrasing: Paraphrasing is an effective communication skill. It indicates that you have understood the complete message and are rephrasing it with your own words. It shows the speaker that you're listening, and that you care enough to make sure you understand what they intended you to hear. It takes some skill, but it is worthwhile to learn and practice, because it is effective. Paraphrasing helps to minimize conflict, and helps to reduce differences between the listener and the speaker. Therefore, it is effective in promoting a better interpersonal relationship.

In the previous section, I have discussed why *active listening* is important, and presented some practical knowledge and skills. The following are other skills essential to successful communication.

UNDERSTAND THE EGO STATE

Psychologist Eric Berne started Transactional Analysis in 1960. He suggested that human beings behave and communicate in three different ego states: *parent, adult and child ego states.* Every communication represents one of the ego states (Berne, 1960). Every communication represents one of ego states. Speaking with the *parent ego state implies authority, power, teaching, command or judgment.* On the other hand, speaking in a *child ego state indicates dependence on an authority figure. The child ego state is a listening party of the parent ego state.* The communication pattern is *childish, playful and irresponsible like a child.* The *adult ego state* communication presents *adult qualities, and is realistic, responsible and mature.* People who communicate with the parent ego state are not always parents, but their speaking pattern or style is authoritarian or powerful. In fact, to support parents in communicating effectively, I encourage *parents to speak to their children (especially to adolescents) in the adult ego state.* With this model, the *child will not remain in the child ego state throughout the developmental stage but will mature into an adult ego state and communicate with parents in a realistic and responsible pattern.*

The following illustration explains the interaction of each ego state in communication: (From Eric Bern, Transactional Analysis in Psychotherapy, 1961)

Ego State;

Parent ego state:	**P**	**Behaviors, thoughts and feelings presenting power, authority – parent figures**
Adult ego state:	**A**	**Behaviors, thoughts and feelings are reasonable, realistic, which are direct response to the here and now**
Child ego state:	**C**	**Behaviors, thoughts and feelings replayed from childhood -- childish**

Here is an example of a conversation pattern, where two people are relating from the parent/child ego states:

Example: **Mother:** "How many times do I have to tell you to put away your shoes?" (Parent ego state, authority).

Son: looks at mother, unwillingly removes shoes

without a word, slams the door (child ego state, childish in nonverbal behavior). *Both parties are unhappy.* Now here is how the same situation, if the mother uses the adult ego to communicate with the child, would be:

Mother: "John, I'd really like to see those shoes put away. They have been there for a while." (Adult ego state comment = realistic and fairly stated.)

John: "Sorry, Mom." And he puts his shoes away. (Adult ego state reaction = responsible.)

The communication can be much more effective if the speaker is *aware of his/her own* ego state in speaking pattern.

Communicating with an *"I" message verses a "You" message*: The purpose of communication is to share information or thoughts or feelings. Nevertheless, it involves two parties — one who talks and the other who listens. Using an "I" message communicates your feelings and shows your perception of the situation. Using a "You" message often suggests blame or criticism. Now, let's try this in the conversation setting, using "I" or "you" in the message, and see what difference it makes:

Example A:

Wife: "**You** didn't come home until midnight and **you** didn't bother to give me a call."

And this is the "I" message for the above case:

Wife: "**I** was wondering what happened to you last night. **I** wished you had called me." The wife's "**I**" message reveals her feelings and needs effectively. In contrast, her **"You"** message seems complaining and blaming.

Example B — Mother talks to her son:

Mother: "**You** are just lazy! This application has been here for three months. **You** are hopeless!"

Mother: "**I** think you are not using your time

effectively. This application has been here for three months. **I** hope you will find time to finish it. Is there a way I can help?"

The mother's "**You**" message indicates criticism and judgment. It only hurts her son's feelings and doesn't have any positive impact on her son. She is also hurting their mother/son relationship. The *"I" message states the fact, and expresses the mother's concern as a suggestion rather than criticism.* It is effective and useful in parent/child relationships.

"**I**" messages are also effective for *delivering a difficult message*, such as in situations of *confrontation*. Most of us are reluctant to confront others, even though we wish to clarify our feelings or thoughts or assert our needs. But how can we *effectively confront others* without hurting each other's feelings? My suggestion for an effective way to begin a confrontation is to use an "I- message", because "I" messages exhibit self-disclosure on the speaker's part, such as feelings or needs. In the above *example A*, the wife confronts her husband's late return. The "I" message expresses her feelings and needs and it sounds sincere to the listener who will then feel encouraged to explain his actions calmly. In contrast, a "You" message often sounds accusatory or complaining, placing the listener in a defensive position.

The above are key concepts which will help you become aware of communication patterns so that you can communicate more clearly and effectively and create more successful relationships. With this basic information in mind, we will move on to the next step: communication with your family members.

Chapter 2
Successful Communication
with Your Young Children

Some people think that because young children don't understand language, it's impossible to communicate with them. Actually, spoken language is merely one kind of communication. There are many other ways to send and receive messages. Communication between mother and child should not be limited because of the child's age; a mother can effectively communicate with her infant child by smiling at her baby. A mother's smile shows her baby the mother's love. This communication implies a relationship, a powerful connection between a helpless infant and a mother who loves the child and understands and meets her child's needs. This chapter is focused on communication with young children from infancy up to age 4.

ACCEPTANCE

Acceptance is a *fundamental concept and attitude* in communicating with your young child.

First, parents need to accept that they are *human, not gods.* Since they are only human, they have to keep learning if they are to become effective and happy parents. The parents who think they are, or ought to be, some kind of "super-beings" will not learn, because of their attitude of superiority. Some people believe that parents ought to know or appear to know everything in the presence of their children. This belief blocks the opportunity for learning about and understanding one's children. In my observation of my clients, I have come to believe that parents can learn a great deal from their children. Yes, we were once children, but we do not remember how it felt to be an infant or a toddler. A famous child psychologist, Jean Piaget, spent many years observing his own child in order to understand the cognitive development of children. Piaget made a great contribution to the field of psychology with his theory of cognitive development. All parents have the same opportunity as Piaget to learn from their children, to watch them grow, to understand their laughter many parents overlook these opportunities. I observed my grandson when he was about seven months old: I was feeding him baby food and gave him another spoon to play with. He threw the spoon on the floor, which made noise, and he was happy and amused by the noise he had made. Then I gave him a small stuffed toy in exchange for the spoon and watched him. He threw the toy on the floor as he did the spoon, but it did not make noise. He was obviously unhappy and wanted the spoon back. He recognized that the stuffed toy would not make noise like the spoon. He did not use language, but we communicated. I understood his happy feeling when he threw the spoon to make noise, and his unhappy feeling when the spoon was changed to the toy which did not do the job he anticipated, so I learned from him about his needs and feelings.

Second, parents need to *accept their children for who they are*, regardless of age, gender and ability. Infants and toddlers have limited spoken language ability. Also, their talents, needs and abilities are individually different. Even siblings raised by the same parent are different from each other. *Accepting who you* *are as parents and who your children are* is the basic foundation for becoming an effective parent and an effective communicator.

Parents who are effective communicators are able to identify and understand their young children's feelings. They are able to appropriately talk about and express feelings to young children. They need to tune in carefully to the child's messages and reflect upon them. For example, when a mother smiles at her baby during feedings, although the baby does not understand language, the mother's smile has meaning while the feeding satisfies the baby's hunger. If the mother smiles sweetly at the baby, the young baby soon begins to associate this feeling of satisfaction with the mother's tender smile. Thus, *communication occurs as the mother shares her feelings of love and care.* She accepts her young baby's communication limitations, and understands her baby's needs. As the baby responds to the mother's care and love, the baby is able to relax in the mother's arms. Later, the baby will learn to smile back at the mother during the feeding. These initial *interactions* between mother and baby are powerful steps in establishing a feeling of mutual acceptance.

When parents are able to communicate their genuine acceptance to their young children, they are opening a door for *trust.* According to Erikson's psychosocial development theory, children at this stage learn and develop a sense of trust. This trust leads children to be unafraid of sharing their feelings. Thus, the door of communication between parents and their young children is opened.

Children need to learn to trust other people, and that trust must begin in the family. During Christmastime, a three-year-old boy came to his mother and asked, "Mommy, please write a letter to Santa for me. I want to be sure Santa remembers what I want, but I can't write." Then he brought his mother a pen and a piece of paper. His mother followed her son's instructions and wrote the letter. The young boy trusted that his mother would do what he needed her to do.

PARENTAL CONFIDENCE

Although parents must accept that they are still learning, they must still develop a sense of confidence in their parenting skills. Confidence as a parent is really just an attitude: you might be an inexperienced parent, but nevertheless you love and care about your child. A loving heart is the most essential element of becoming a confident, effective parent and an effective communicator with a young child. Your confidence helps establish your child's trust. Your young child will share your confidence and grow happily with you. Parents' confidence makes children comfortable about themselves and the environment they are in, and the children feel secure and at ease. That confidence helps the young children engage in communication without fear, expressing their thoughts and feelings and asking questions, even though their language ability is limited.

Example: A ten-month-old baby watched his father turn on the light with a switch, and he was curious about the switch. He wished to touch it, but could not express his wish verbally. Luckily, his father understood the boy's desire and held him up to reach the switch. He helped the little boy turn the light on and off, and that created excitement. Then the father allowed him to try it by himself, and he was thrilled by this new experience. The parent understood the boy's desire, and allowing him to turn the switch on and off was a simple non-verbal communication between the parent and the child. That kind of communication helps develop self-confidence, trust, and a sense of autonomy which are important tasks for small children to learn at this stage.

HOW TO ESTABLISH COMMUNICATION SUCCESSFULLY WITH SMALL CHILDREN

1. Play: Play is an important part of a child's life. Children share their needs, thoughts and feelings during playtime. They acquire new knowledge and social skills through play. To young children, play is a way of communicating. Parent and child communication starts at an early stage by playing together. When you, as a parent, take time *to play with your young child, you are communicating* your messages of love and care to your child. Your child learns and enjoys his/her childhood because you communicate with your child by playing with him/her. During playtime, using simple vocabulary combined with motions such as nodding your head or giving a hug builds your child's confidence and self-esteem. Your encouragement of your child with comments like "Good job!" or "Great!" will bring a smile to your child's face. We use simple language in playing with young children to help them develop and improve language skills. Didn't we learn phrases like "thank you" and "you are welcome" from our parents when we were young children?

I have found from my clinical experience that when children are identified as "problem kids," the problem is often that their parents seldom spent enough time playing with them. Today's parents are very busy with their work, so that taking time out to play with their children doesn't seem to be a high priority. This is a sad mistake, because they do not realize how much they and their children miss by failing to spend time playing together. They fail to recognize that playtime is a *parent/child communication time*. Through play, the foundation of a precious young life is laid, and effective communication is taught and learned. Since both the parent and the child learn from each other and share time and activity, play is essential to parent/child relationships.

Play is an effective communication tool. It is so powerful that therapists use play as a therapeutic approach to resolve many of the psychological problems that young children have. Play therapy is an effective way to identify a young client's unspoken feelings and thoughts. Through interactions during the play sessions, the therapist engages in communication with the child, both verbal and nonverbal. The therapist listens to the child's *feelings,* such as *hurt, scared, sad or lonely*. These feelings may be expressed in a simple form of language (baby talk) or even through playing with a doll or a game. Nevertheless, they are communication, and the therapist listens attentively and accepts whatever the child communicates. The therapeutic intervention begins with *rapport and genuine caring.* Although the children may be unable to express their feelings or describe situations with spoken language, they can communicate clearly using their own methods. They are unafraid to communicate with the therapist because of the bond of trust between them.

Example: A pre-school teacher referred a student, a four-year-old boy named Billy, to my clinic. The major concern was that Billy used to be a happy, popular boy in school, but he had recently become a quiet and grouchy boy, and was not participating in any activities. Then he got worse, pushing and attacking other children. At home, his mother noticed he was not eating as much as he used to. The mother admitted that she did not have the time and energy to pay attention to him. During the initial play session, Billy was very quiet and looked down. I told him that his teacher and his parents were worried about him, because he was not as happy as he had been. They wondered what made him change into an unhappy boy. I told him I wanted to be his friend—a grownup friend. And I wanted to see him happy like he was before. He looked at me and said, "You don't understand, I am very sad," and looked down again. I said to him, "I don't understand now, but would you like to tell me about it? Then I might understand. Usually I am pretty good at understanding children. I have many young friends like you, who are your age." He paused for a while, and said, "See, I have lost a baby brother." Then he went on to tell me that his mother was pregnant for seven months but unfortunately the baby was stillborn. Apparently, Billy's mother had a hard time carrying a pregnancy to full term, and this pregnancy had been a big hope for Billy and his parents. Billy was really anticipating a baby brother to play with. But his parents went to the hospital and returned with the sad news that they had lost the baby. Billy's parents were very sad and cried. The whole family was in a depressed mood, but the parents expected Billy to be unaffected and remain in the same mood: playing, eating and going to school as usual. Billy did not have any opportunity to express his sadness or share his parents' feelings as a family member. After Billy's play session, I invited his mother in, and asked her about the unfortunate pregnancy. She was surprised that the incident had affected Billy's mental health and influenced his behavior. She had believed the loss was an adult's business, and that her son should not be involved or affected, and thus she completely ignored Billy's feelings. I explained to her the importance of respecting him as a member of the family regardless of his age — just as he was informed of the pregnancy, he should have been informed of the miscarriage, thus indicating the value of his place within the family. This is a good example of why family communication is so important. After I explained this to the mother, I scheduled a family play session, and helped mother and son to express their feelings regarding their loss of the baby. During the play session, Billy's mother had an opportunity to apologize to her son while they were playing the sand-box. Billy was very understanding; he nodded his head, indicating he accepted his mother's feelings. This is successful communication between mother and son while they were playing together. Since then, Billy's teacher informed me that Billy has become a happy boy again.

Clear and open communication is vital between family members, regardless of their age. In the above example, Billy's household included only the parents and a young child. The situation might have been different if Billy had had a grandmother or an older sibling in his family with whom he could have shared and expressed his feelings. Nevertheless, even if children are young and have limited knowledge, when parents respect their needs they will be confident in sharing their feelings.

2) Recognizing or rewarding the young child's success or good behavior is an effective way to establish the child's positive self-image. Some cultures and families believe that praising a child's success at a young age will spoil the child and lead him to become too proud in the future. However, I firmly believe that if the recognition or praise is based on *truth and is justified* (that is, the praise is *not an exaggeration* but a *genuine message* to the child), it does not spoil the child, but expresses a parent's enjoyment of the child's accomplishment. This is a positive family communication. Effective parents give unconditional positive regard to their young child, realizing that though their children are limited in many areas such as language, knowledge and physical strength, they are still learning and developing every moment. As parents, we accept our children the way they are, understand their limited conditions, and encourage and support them. We have to give empathic listening ears to their limited vocabulary and language skill, and talk to them with simple but clear expressions. This kind of parent/child communication provides the child an opportunity to develop spontaneity because the child feels confident, which is essential for self-growth in adulthood.

An effective parent will recognize when their child is ready to grow, and respond appropriately. Three-year-old Melissa was holding a book, imitating her five-year-old sister's reading. Her mother noticed, and realized that Melissa wished to read like her sister. Here was the mother's comment to Melissa: "Wow! Melissa, you sound so good and look just like your sister. I know you wish you could read. How about if you sit holding the book and Mommy reads and you follow, okay?" Melissa followed her mother's reading and they both enjoyed the experience. What would be your reaction if you were Melissa's parent?

3) *Nonverbal Communication* is important at all ages, but especially so when interacting with young children. A toddler or an infant may not have well developed verbal skills as yet; nevertheless, they do listen to our tone of voice and watch our facial

expressions and body language as we talk to them. Soon they recognize (read) our feelings through nonverbal communication. This is the essential first step of communication that they learn from the adults around them. Young babies have a natural self-protective sense that lets them know whether they are safe. A gentle smile and a soft voice makes them calm and relaxed. An angry face and loud noises will frighten them. Without understanding a word, our babies know how we feel. The baby responds by crying after seeing an angry facial expression or hearing a loud voice, or even after carefully studying a stranger's face. This crying is a message that the baby is feeling frightened. If parents are able to comfort and assure the child that he or she is in good hands, the baby will be able to regain a feeling of peace, and relax. Every child knows that a smiling face comes from a happy feeling and is a sign of approval.

Likewise, young babies soon learn which gestures and facial expressions convey disapproval. From the first time parents hold their newborn, they begin to learn to interpret the meanings of their child's various cries. Infants too, quickly learn to understand their parents' nonverbal messages. Thus, *effective communication begins in the family from the moment of birth.*

In order to provide a secure, healthy and happy environment for their children, parents must constantly seek to improve their communication skills and take care to communicate their love and care to their young child, and to meet their child's needs by understanding the verbal and nonverbal messages that their child is communicating. It is helpful for the parents to learn and practice positive nonverbal messages, such as *hugging, kissing, smiling, winking, putting an arm around the child's shoulders and affectionately rubbing their hair.*

PROTECTING CHILDREN FROM ADULT CONFLICT

Sometimes the adults and/or parents in a child's life are in conflict with each other, and the child feels *caught between them.* Often, the conflict is communicated to the child verbally and nonverbally, leading the child to feel confused and distressed. Unfortunately, parents are often unaware that their child is being hurt by their harmful communications. Children may feel that they have caused the conflict or they may feel responsible for fixing it. Such conflicts can stem from marital difficulties or other hidden family issues.

Example: A four-year-old girl, Betty, lived with her parents, who had a rough marriage and finally divorced. After the divorce, Betty lived with her mother and visited her father on weekends. Each time Betty returned from her father's, her mother would ask a lot of questions. The questions were so complicated that

Betty could not respond. Then her mother would get upset and complain that Betty was not nice to her and was not on her side. The little girl was caught in the middle of her parents' conflict. Betty became moody at her preschool and cried a lot. Her mother also reported that Betty often had nightmares and cried during the night. Betty was referred for play therapy. During the play session, Betty cried and told her therapist that she loved her mother and also loved her father, and that she missed her father, but hesitated to visit him, because she was scared that her mother would ask those hard questions again. During the interview with Betty's mother, the therapist found that Betty's mother had been hurt so much from the divorce that she did not realize how much she had involved her daughter in her marriage and her divorce. Subsequently, Betty's mother was helped by her therapist to resolve her personal issues and adjust to her divorce. Betty's mother finally realized that her young daughter had been hurt because she was caught in the middle of her parents' marriage conflict.

This was the conversation at a family play-session. Betty's mother told Betty: "I know you love mommy and you also love your daddy. But your dad moved out and we are divorced now, because we didn't want to live together. We fought all the time. But one thing I want to tell you, and I want you to remember. Daddy and mommy still love you the same way, and you will be taken care of the same way." Betty nodded her head. Betty's mom put Betty on her lap, and Betty put her arms around her mom's neck and turned to her mom and smiled. Play with young children is a powerful and effective way to open the door to communication.

I have noticed that when most adults talk to each

other or argue with each other at home, we often don't notice our children beside us. In the above two examples, Billy and Betty had caring mothers, but they did not initially pay attention to their children's feelings and needs. We adults often think young children don't understand what we are talking about. It is true that they have limited language skills, and their limited cognitive ability doesn't allow them to comprehend adult issues. Nevertheless, we cannot ignore the young child as a family member. We can use simple language or nonverbal communication such as drawing pictures or using puppets to provide an opportunity for children to express their feelings. Adults may also explain their situations to young children with an open attitude and at an age-appropriate level. The most important point is that the parents assure their young children that they are loved and cared for, no matter what the situation is.

Chapter 3
Communicating Successfully
with Preteen School-Age Children

In this chapter the discussion is focused on school-age children, from five through twelve years of age. During this developmental stage, children are eager to learn. Their cognitive abilities greater and their language skills are increasing. They have an increased ability to express ideas, to develop logical thinking, and to explore. Because of their increasing language ability, they become sociable and have the opportunity to interact with other children at school every day. School also provides them with new knowledge, and challenges their intellectual development. All of these new skills and knowledge make the school-age children seem more like small adults. They are becoming enjoyable children. This period is regarded as a fun stage for parents and children. Nevertheless, it is an important stage for developing a proper foundation of effective communication. In order to meet their child's development needs, parents of these children need to consider that the home environment provides a model of effective communication. This chapter explores particular approaches which help to provide that model.

COMMUNICATE TRUTH

Children at this stage have a greater sense of morality. They develop interest in rules and order and they increase the capacity of self-regulation as they grow. Parents need to be aware of their child's developmental process, and demonstrate to their children that parents are speaking *truth.* However, many parents are *unaware of when they are not speaking the truth.* In this culture, we accept "white lies" or exaggerations of the truth as a common practice of getting along in society. This may not seem to be a big offense, but it's an important pattern to notice, since children are listening and learning, and will eventually imitate our communication and behavior.

Example: In a family session, a mother was complaining to the therapist that her husband *never* helped with housework or took care of the children. Her eight-year-old daughter, Joan, who was listening, looked at her mother, and said: "That's not true! He washed dishes sometimes, and he took me to the dentist last week, remember? Mom!" Joan was protesting her mother's exaggeration.

Parents provide models. If we want our children to

learn the right thing and tell the truth, we have to show them that model. In the above example, the mother was exaggerating. It was not a real "lie", but for an eight-year-old, it seemed like one, so she protested that it was not "true." Then, after her mother said, "Sorry, dear. That was mom's overstatement. I meant that your father does not like to help with house chores. Is that true? " her daughter nodded her head. I encourage parents to acknowledge their mistakes, so their children may learn this healthy attitude from the parents. It is not always easy to admit our own mistakes — it takes courage to do so — and that is why school-age children need a good model to learn from.

THE CONTENT OF COMMUNICATION MUST BE CONSISTENT AND CLEAR. AVOID AMBIGUITY

Children at this age are developing logical thinking and are fully attentive in listening when an adult's words are interesting to them. But when they find the message in an adult's conversation inconsistent or ambiguous, they feel confused, and they may lose interest or lose trust in the adult's communication. When we communicate, we reflect or reveal our inner selves. School-age children are developing their self-esteem during this stage of life. If they see that the adults around them are in conflict or are inconsistent, or have double standards in communication, the children may lose trust in adults. They may also become insecure, and be unable to find a proper model from which to learn communication.

Example: One day Fred was busy doing paperwork in his study. His ten-year-old son, Ted, came in and said, "Dad, telephone. He said his name is Jack". The father appeared irritated and said, "Oh, no, tell him I am not home." His son was sort of puzzled, and started to ask, "But, dad…" His father responded, *"Just do what I said!"* Ted left the room and returned to the phone, and *did what his father said*, but he was not comfortable because *his father was lying*. His father had always told his children, *"Don't lie."* Ted was disturbed by *his father's double standard* of behavior. Ted went to his mother and shared his feelings with her. His mother explained to him that his father was working hard to meet the deadline of the caller, Jack. When Jack called, Fred was not ready; therefore he avoided talking to Jack. Ted's mother explained this much, but she encouraged Ted to clarify the situation further with his father and express his feelings and thoughts. Ted's mother kept an objective and supportive attitude, and provided Ted an opportunity to learn a positive model of confrontation and to establish a healthy communication pattern in the family. Preteen children are very good at noticing inconsistency and ambiguity in their own families. Have you heard or had a similar story similar to Ted's family? If you were Ted's mother, what would you do?

UNDERSTAND THAT SCHOOL-AGE CHILDREN ARE AT THE STAGE OF DEVELOPING FEELINGS

These emotions include empathy, love, compassion and sharing as well as feelings of fear, fairness, guilt and anger. Despite developing more complicated feelings, school-age children are still in a stage that is relatively relaxed and free of conflict. They are able to enjoy family and peers. They like to join in family conversation and listen to the adults talk. Their language skills have increased to a level where they enjoy being with peers, talking and listening to each other's thoughts and feelings. Therefore, they enjoy friendship at school and companionship with family members at home. They are learning to improve the effectiveness of communication from *their own experience and with the support of the family* and *friends*. As adults, we have to understand that children at this age are developing their sense of feelings, and are more willing to learn. We should provide the proper opportunity and guidance to meet their needs. One effective way to establish communication with school-age children is to *work together with them to solve their problem*, as illustrated in the following.

Example: A friend of mine was driving her nine-year-old son, David, to his violin lesson. On the way, they saw a man taking care of a big dog at the roadside. The dog appeared to be injured, and the man was with the dog and appeared to be helping. Both David and his mother knew that they were not able to participate in helping the dog, because they had an appointment with the violin teacher, but David felt bad about not being able to help. But David's mother quickly told him, "As soon as we get to your teacher's office, I will call the police station and report what we have seen, and the policeman can arrange for help. The dog will get help. We will try our best to get help for that dog." David's mother talked to him with *assurance*. David seemed to appreciate his mother's idea. David's mother was a considerate mother. She understood her son's tender, sensitive feelings and she supported her son's growth in developing his sense of feelings. As soon as David finished his violin lesson, he rushed to his mother and asked, "What happened to the dog?" With smile on her face, my friend answered, "Oh, a policeman went to help them, and took the dog to a vet. He said the dog had some cuts, but he will be all right." As David sighed and felt relieved, he hugged his mom.

Parents of school-age children have many opportunities to be with their children, and therefore they need to understand the developmental task of this stage: parents have to *keep the communication open* and be able to *listen* and *share* their thoughts and feelings. This stage is a great time for children to *learn how to find a proper solution*. David worried that the dog was left there, and his mother understood his feelings. His mother supported David's feelings; at the same time, his mother taught him an *appropriate way to resolve the problem*.

LISTEN AND TALK TO SCHOOL-AGE CHILDREN WITH THE RESPECT THEY DESERVE

Some adults ignore children and do not pay attention, listen, or talk to children with the same respect that they do with adults. Matthew McKay, in his book "Message: The Communication Book"(

Mckay,Davis,Fanning, 1995) described this kind of attitude as "*adult chauvinism.*" Unfortunately, there are many parents who have this attitude—they believe their children are young and inexperienced, and therefore *their feelings are not significant or important.* However, if the parents are effective parents, they will talk to their children with respect, considering their feelings and thoughts. Parental attitudes in communicating with their children are very important *at any time, on any occasion and in any circumstance during their children's lives.* They are *particularly* important during the preteen years, because children at this age are eager to learn and love to interact with people—they are building their *self-esteem.* Parental understanding and respectful communication encourage the children to open up by asking questions or discussing issues with their parents. On the other hand, if the parent ignores the child or make negative remarks during the communication, such as dismissing the child's ideas or feelings, or belittling the child, the child will be hurt. This can also negatively affect the relationship between the parent and the child. The previous example of Fred and his son, Tim, is a good example. Tim almost lost his respect for his father. Fortunately, Tim's mother was instrumental in encouraging Tim to communicate with his father.

Our children need our support to grow and learn, and we as parents also need to grow and learn with them. The following is another example.

Example: Matt is a 10-year-old boy. He is the second child in his family, with one brother who is four years older than he is. Matt's mother brought him for counseling at the suggestion of his teacher. The teacher's main concerns were that Matt was not paying attention and not doing well at school. Matt's mother provided the following information during her interview with the therapist, while Matt was present.

Mother: "*I wish Matt were as smart as his older brother (sigh)*. My older son is doing so well in school that his room is filled with awards and ribbons. But this one (pointing to Matt), not even one! First of all, *during my pregnancy I wished for a girl*, but I got a boy. I was totally disappointed, but *I had to stick with him*. Then, he gave me all these headaches." She paused. "I don't know what to do."

Therapist: "You sound disappointed, like you are feeling helpless, but you still care about your son. You just don't know how to help him."

Mother: "Exactly! Would you help me to do that?"

Therapist: "Yes, I will, but *you* and I and Matt will be all *working together*. You need to learn to *understand him* better, and Matt will learn to do better at school. He will be happier both at home and at school. And you will also learn how to *motivate* your son, and you will enjoy him more." Matt's mother seemed to be relieved by the therapist's assurance.

This mother was not an uncaring mother, but rather *unaware of her own issues*. She was not aware that she was blaming Matt for not being a girl, and for not being as smart as his brother. *Matt's mother put Matt down and robbed him of his self-esteem without realizing it*. Matt's *feelings were hurt*, because he was *not a welcomed baby*. He *did not have confidence* in studying, because he believed that he was not smart, not good enough for anything. The mother's *insensitive messages* affected her son. Matt lost the motivation to learn, and therefore he had no interest in school. His mother was shocked when the therapist helped her discover her mistake. She regretted that her ignorance had affected Matt's self-esteem and had negatively influenced his schoolwork. The therapist gave Matt's mother some therapeutic assignments. One of them was to list Matt's strengths and the good things people said about him. From these assignments Matt's mother realized her son had many strengths that she had not recognized before. She found that Matt had many athletic gifts, so she encouraged him to join a soccer team. Matt played well, his teammates liked him, and he was one of the most valuable players on his team. His whole family, including his father and brother, went to watch his games and cheered him on. They applauded him. Matt was very happy.

Another suggestion that the therapist gave Matt's mother was a list of *positive feedback* sentences to use. Positive feedback promotes the child's self-esteem and confidence so the child will feel he/she is important and respected. The following are some examples of positive feedback:

1. Great! Wow! Good Job! Nice Job! Super! Fantastic! Beautiful! Bravo! Well done!

2. I am very proud of you when you….

3. You are very special! You are amazing! I'm impressed!

4. Thank you for your help. What a great idea! You're sharp!

5. Good for you! Keep up the good work. Good try, you have done a lot better today!

We all need encouragement, no matter what our age or situation in life. But because children at this age are developing their self-esteem, and are so willing to learn, parents need to take particular care at this stage to support the child's developing sense of self. Respect each child as a person and encourage their efforts to develop their potential.

Chapter 4
Communication with
Your Adolescent Children

Adolescence, *from age 13 to 18, is a crucial stage.* At this stage your child is developing into an adult. During these years children are learning how to be adults, yet in some ways they are still children, depending on their parents for providing food, shelter and clothing as well as health care and education. Adolescents are not ready for independent living, but they and their parents and the adults around them are noticing changes in their physical development, Adolescents may have mixed feelings about these changes: feelings of curiosity, excitement and embarrassment. Parents and other adults also have reactions or responses. Some parents may be happy and excited that their children are growing into adulthood. Others may carelessly tease the young person about their appearance. One boy told me he had stopped going to his church because some of the adults at the church often made annoying remarks about his physical changes and his appearance. These comments made him feel uneasy and embarrassed. Adolescence is a difficult stage. In order to effectively communicate with your adolescent children, you need to understand what adolescence is all about.

UNDERSTANDING ADOLESCENCE: THE DEVELOPMENTAL TASKS AND NEEDS OF ADOLESCENTS.

Adolescence is a stage in which the individual develops a self-image and self-identity, not easy tasks. Because teenagers need to build self-identity, they are sensitive to other people's comments. They care about how they appear to others, about their looks, their performance and their interactions with others. Another important task for adolescents is learning to *make their own decisions. Becoming more independent from their parents is quite a challenge.* They no longer want to go to mom and dad for answers or directions; instead, they prefer to find the answers themselves or to ask their peers. As they *struggle with their identity;* their minds are *full of ideas, dreams and uncertainties.* Many parents would agree that their adolescent children can seem quite confused at times. Because of their limited experience in life, adolescents may have a hard time making the right decision at first. They need a great deal of support from *understanding parents* in order to master the tasks of adolescence.

Because adolescence is an identity formation stage,

it is a crucial stage, and difficult in terms of physiological, psychological and social changes. Parents of adolescents are also struggling. They used to be "mommy" and "daddy" and make decisions and give directions to their children. Now they seem to have lost their jobs. Of course the parents are confused and uncertain! As parents, we have to understand that our teenagers are learning to be adults, and that it takes time to grow, so we have to be patient. Since this stage can be the most difficult time for a parent/child relationship, it may not be easy to effectively communicate with your adolescent children. However, there is a positive side to adolescence. Teens have accumulated a great deal of knowledge and their language skills are much more developed, so if parents are understanding and treat them with proper respect, both parent and child will mutually enjoy each other's company, and learn from each other. See if the following example of the challenges of communication in this age group sounds familiar to you.

Example: At 17 years old, Joe is a fully grown adolescent. According to Joe's mother, Joe has stayed in his room more and more, and has spent less and less time with his parents. His mother has noticed that Joe pays more attention to his appearance—he often looks at himself in a mirror and is concerned about his acne. Joe spends more time washing up and putting medicine on his face. Joe's father dislikes Joe's behavior, believing that a boy who pays too much attention to his appearance is "a sissy". Joe's father often teases him, and has made derogatory remarks about his behavior. His father's insensitive attitude and unnecessary remarks toward his adolescent son have badly damaged the father's relationship with Joe. Joe started by ignoring his father. Then he gradually stopped talking to his father. Joe's father has become very upset, and complains, "I lost a son." But Joe's father does not recognize his own role in this deterioration of their relationship. When I met with Joe, he said, "My father does not understand. He just wants to control me, but I need to grow. I am not a little boy any more." Joe looked sad, and he continued, "I don't know what to do." He sighed. "In my opinion, adolescents' parents should be happy to watch their children grow and should wish for children to become successful adults. But my parents often overlook or ignore my growth. I need to reach both physical and emotional maturity. My father doesn't understand all that!"

What a sad experience for both Joe and his parents. However, during my conversation with Joe, I sensed that Joe is pretty mature for his age, and that he understood the situation clearly. Although he has good insight, he did not know *how* to change the situation. *I listened to him attentively*, and *acknowledged his knowledge and his insight*. As our conversation went on, I could see him becoming more comfortable in expressing his feelings. I encouraged him to try talking with his parents. He said he would start with his mother because he thought his mother was more understanding than his father. He told his mom that he was worried about his acne, and his open attitude and honest sharing touched his mother's feelings. They had a good talk that evening. With his mother's support, Joe decided to make an appointment with a dermatologist to take care of his acne. Joe's father also gradually accepted him, and the family's communication improved.

In this case, the improvement in the situation was initiated by the adolescent, which is rather unique. I encouraged Joe to initiate the communication, because I noticed that Joe had a good understanding of the situation, and he said he *wanted to improve the family communication*. He did a good job.

Joe's parents felt hopeless when Joe started to close himself off and did not want to talk to his father. Both his father and mother were sad, but they did not know what to do, and came to see me. Fortunately, Joe initiated the communication with his parents, but usually the parents have to initiate it. As we discussed at the beginning of the chapter, even though adolescents are growing and changing physically, *they are still children*, and parents need the patience to help them learn to be mature. If the parent/child communication is stuck as it was with Joe and his father, it may be that the parent needs to let go of some of his authority, to stop communicating from the parent ego state, and "step down" in order to let his son "step up" into more autonomy. That way, Joe can learn how to be in an adult ego state when he talks to his father. I assume that all parents have helped their children to walk and to climb up the stairs when they were younger. In the same way, your adolescent needs your help and you as parents need to initiate communication to bring adolescents into the circle of family communication again.

TRUST AND RESPECT

Parental respect and trust are crucial issues in adolescents' lives. Trust and respect are symbols of parental recognition, and show that the parents support their child's growth. Trust and respect *enhance an adolescent's confidence*, enable him to *go forward and face challenges*, and while he is experiencing the challenge, *help him to develop critical thinking*. It's also important to facilitate young people's *enjoyment of the adolescent stage so they are happy to move on to adulthood.* When the parent and the adolescent child have *mutual trust and respect,* they are able to communicate with each other from the adult ego state (refer to Chapter One, Key Concepts), which means they are *realistic and reasonable.* Then, both parent and adolescent can enjoy their communication.

LETTING GO

The physical growth of adolescents is so rapid that some *parents are not prepared* for such quick changes. These physical changes may make parents uneasy: they see their children growing up, and realize that they are no longer little children, but will be soon leaving home, and possibly getting married. Some parents may be *afraid of losing* their children, and *reluctant to let go of* their adolescent child. These parents may be *controlling their children's growth without realizing it.*

Example: An only son of a single mother, Jason is 19 years old. He was an excellent student. After he graduated from high school, Jason was awarded a full scholarship to an Ivy League university, but his mother would not let him go because he would have to move to another state. Jason felt sad and disappointed, but he did not know what to do, because Jason's mother *would not listen to nor talk* with Jason.

Jason's mother was not aware that she was blocking her son's growth. If she could share her feelings and concerns with Jason, Jason could express his disappointment at the same time. When I had a long talk with Jason's mother, she revealed that she could not let her son go because she was worried that she would miss him. She felt secure when he was near her. Her insecurity and her *lack of self-confidence* was her own issue, and that was causing her to hold her son back. She said she wanted her son to be successful, yet she had a hard time making the decision to let Jason go. Jason's mother knew and admitted that Jason would be all right at the university, if only she could let go! I encouraged her to talk with Jason and to listen to his thoughts and feelings. She had to be open and honest in order to develop good communication between them. She needed to remember that she is the mother, and that her son needed her support to grow. Jason's mother wanted her son to receive that scholarship and get a good education, yet she was not *ready to let her adolescent son go*, and she needed time to realize that. I was just in time to support her "letting go" process.

CARE AND LOVE

Adolescents are growing fast in many areas; nevertheless, *they need their parents' care and love*. The methods of caring and loving may be different than when they were younger. One significant difference is that the parents must be *willing to step down*, or to give up having complete authority for their children, and allow their adolescent children to *step up*, or to take on more authority for their own lives. This attitude comes from parental *understanding, trust and respect*. If parents and adolescents are able to reach this level, then adolescents can communicate with people at the *adult ego level*.

Parental care and love support adolescents to make decisions, or to be able to discuss their opinions with parents. It is true that the young person is inexperienced—they may make mistakes, and that is a *learning process*. Every young person has to go through this learning process to reach maturity, just as we have learned from many mistakes throughout our lives. When your adolescent child makes a mistake or a wrong decision, do not quickly condemn her/him, but listen to her/him in order to understand *how* the decision was made. This is important for the adolescent as well as for the parent—to *understand the decision process*. This understanding includes the *consequences of the decision*. Adolescents need parental care and love, not criticism or discouragement, to grow into successful adults.

Example: Wayne was a sophomore college student. He had a car that his parents had bought for him. He liked his car and took good care of it. One day, a friend rode with him and forgot to lock the door, and his precious car radio was stolen. That radio was very special because he had bought it with his savings from his summer job. Wayne was very upset. The thief also did some damage to the car, so he had to tell his parents about it and needed to deal with the insurance company. It was not an easy task for Wayne, but when his father noticed some uneasiness in Wayne, he nicely initiated the question, "Wayne, are you okay?" which helped Wayne to open up and explain the situation. Wayne's father calmed him down and guided him to accept the mistake, and said this could be a valuable experience for him. Then his father helped him talk to the insurance agent and took him to the car dealer. Wayne's father was right—Wayne learned a lot from this incident. Now Wayne is a successful executive with a large company. He often shares this experience with others. Wayne said his father's love and care had contributed to his success today. His father's guidance during his adolescence helped him make decisions, built self-confidence and helped him grow into successful adulthood.

ENJOY YOUR ADOLESCENT CHILDREN AND GROW WITH THEM

Be open-minded and celebrate the fact that your many years of hard work are paying off now! Your child is an adolescent, in an exciting stage; nevertheless, it is an important stage. The parenting of teens is different from parenting younger children—it is a challenging role and a difficult task, but it can be rewarding, because your child will soon be an adult. That should be a happy thought.

You've already noticed that your adolescent child's knowledge has increased, and language ability is remarkably improved. This is a time to enjoy talking and listening to your teenage child, to learn more about the young person and to share each other's feelings, thoughts and opinions. Having an adolescent at home is like having another adult living at home. You can communicate with your adolescent child on an *adult ego* level—you can exchange ideas, and share each other's dreams. Parents may share (but not lecture) about their life experience, their *successes and failures*.

This helps young adults understand that everyone succeeds sometimes, and fails sometimes. The adult also needs to be opened-minded and willing to listen and share with the adolescent.

I heard a joking remark once, suggesting that you should I "Bury your child at age 13, and dig him out at 18". In my opinion, the age between 13 through 18 are precious and enjoyable, if parents can appreciate the growth and development of their adolescent. They are maturing and full of energy, they are sensible and articulate individuals. Now we will get into the discussion of *how* to communicate with your teenager.

HOW TO COMMUNICATE EFFECTIVELY WITH YOUR ADOLESCENT

1. To be an effective listener, be an attentive listener: sincerely listen to the adolescent's message. Sometimes the message is a cry for help. We often hear about rebellious acts of adolescent children; these are another way of communication, of sending adults, parents or society their messages and feelings. Betty, the adolescent runaway described at the beginning of this book, could not communicate with her parents. Because they would not listen, and she did not know how to make them understand her, running away was the only way to express her feelings.

An effective listener provides response and acknowledgment. Responses can be nonverbal, such as nodding the head or warmly looking into the adolescent's eyes, or verbal, such as saying "I am sorry" or "I'm glad you're telling me this." These are signs of support and acknowledgment.

2. Initiate communication: Adolescents are often unable to initiate communication, either because they are not used to initiating the discussion, or because they are not allowed to initiate due to the culture in which they were brought up. Adults need to provide opportunities and encouragement for teens to initiate communication. Genuine understanding and patience are the keys which allow adults to play this role. Many therapists and counselors are able to help adolescents open up. They establish rapport with adolescent clients because of their sincere interest in them and by patiently waiting for the young person to initiate communication. The previous example of Wayne's father is a good example of sincere interest.

3. Ask questions that encourage conversation: Use *open-ended* questions and avoid questions that call for a yes or no answer. *Avoid investigative question*s, such as, "Where did you go? Or what did you do?" Such questions sound like a policeman investigating a case. An adolescent client once told me that he was certain that every time he returned home from an outing, his mother would ask where he went. "Whom did you go with?" "What did you do there?" He said, "I knew exactly what my mother would ask. I remembered all my mother's questions. I can follow her questions one after another, just like a recorded tape, and it's so funny! Sometime I feel I don't have to listen to her, because I know the rest of her message, so I turn off!"

Here is an example of an open-ended question which the mother could ask when her son returned from a different city:

Mother: "I'm glad you are back. Tell me about that city. I've never been there and I'm eager to know about it."

Communication in the family is not as effective when it's "routine". We want to have communication that *connects us to each other.* Many parents ask questions like "How was school?" The children's answer is often "Fine," and that's it. The communication ends. Here is an example of engaging the adolescent in more conversation.

Example: A woman's 16-year-old son, Ted, returns from school.

Mother: "So, how was your term paper, Ted? Did you turn it in today?"

Ted: "I did. A few people asked the teacher for an extension, though."

Mother: "Wow, I'm glad you finished in time. I thought your topic, 'History of Africa', sounded very interesting. I noticed you were searching for information on the internet. Did you find something good?"

Ted: "Yes, and I found some really cool stuff from *National Geographic.* That was also interesting."

A more specific question usually invites conversation. Adolescents appreciate their parents showing genuine interest in their projects or work.

Open-ended questions with genuine care and interest will keep meaningful communication moving along with your adolescent.

4. Be self-aware when you communicate with your adolescents. Notice your own feelings and needs, your values, and your experiences, either positive or negative. These are part of your "self", and may affect your communication with your adolescents. A judgmental attitude or response can damage the effectiveness of your communication. A common example is the parent who says, "You don't know how lucky you are! When we were your age...." This may be an unfair statement, because the parent is not considering the differences of the times and environment. Thus, this is an *ineffective parent/child communication.* Parents need to be aware of generational differences, and need to be considerate.

An effective way is to enter discussion with your adolescent with an open mind, thus *establishing two-way communication*, and to *listen to each other's opinion*s. With an open-minded attitude you can share your experiences—either your successes or failures—with your adolescent. And you and your adolescent can learn from each other.

5. *Avoid comparing your adolescent child with others*. Here is an example: A father said to his adolescent son, Jim, "Look at Henry, the boy next door. *He is so responsible*. His father told me that Henry received an admission letter from MIT. *Why can't you be like him*?" Jim's father probably did not intend to hurt him or put him down, but still Jim was hurt. Jim did not respond to his father, but quietly went to his room. Adolescence is a sensitive stage, and *self-identity* is a crucial issue at this developmental stage. Careless

remarks or unnecessary comparisons can cause tremendous damage, because they affect the adolescent's feelings and self image. Parents often damage the relationship between themselves and their teenagers without realizing it because of ineffective communication skills. Some parents intentionally praise other people's children to inspire their own children to do better. This is not a healthy approach. I recommend that parents encourage their adolescent children and accept them for who they are. Parental understanding and caring are real groundwork for your child's success. If a teenager's parents praise another teenager, it only discourages their own children and hurts their self-esteem. However, if your son brings a friend home and you observe that the friend has good qualities, you can comment on his good qualities and encourage your son to continue the friendship. Then you could say, "Your

friend seems nice. It's good to have a friend like him."
This doesn't discourage your son or put him down.

6. Use "I" messages in communicating with your adolescents: In most families, parents are "insiders" in terms of family situations, such as family finances, future plans, etc. Parents often plan together without their children's participation. Therefore, children are not always aware of family situations, even when their parents are having a problem. If parents wish to involve their teenage children in order to provide an opportunity to be responsible and to prepare them for adulthood, parental self-disclosure is helpful. An effective method of self-disclosure is to use "I" messages in communication. An "I" message is self-expressive and implies sincere feeling. "I" messages should not indicate authority, instruction or control. In communicating with teenagers, "I" messages are more effective and appropriate than "you" messages. Because adolescents are struggling for self-identity and self-confidence, "I" messages make them feel they are respected and recognized. As a result of your modeling, adolescents themselves will use "I" messages in communicating with others as well.

As I have described previously, "I" messages are also effective in communicating during confrontation. This is especially important because confronting your adolescent child may not be a pleasant job.

Both self-disclosure and confrontation are difficult messages to deliver, especially to adolescents, because their feelings can be sensitive.

The following examples indicate two different situations:

Example 1. A father shares his concern with his 18-year-old son, Steve.

Father: "Steve, I'd like to share my concern with you. Your mother's doctor has done an extensive exam on her breast and he said it could be cancer. She's pretty tired, and we're waiting for the final decision, so *I need your support*. Please help your mom, if you can."

Steve: "I will, dad. I'm sorry to hear this. I hope Mom will be all right. Dad, I could check my brother's homework, so Mom doesn't need to be bothered."

Father: "That's a great idea. Thank you, Steve. I know I can depend on you."

Steve: "Dad, please keep me posted. I'd like to help as much as I can. Please don't keep all the worries to yourself."

Father: "You are great! Son, I will tell you when her doctor decides on the treatment plan."

Steve's father used "I" messages to disclose the family's problem, and Steve responded responsibly.

This is an illustration of effective communication between a father and his teenage son. It also illustrates a cohesive family. Adolescent children are members of the family.

Example 2: A 15-year-old adolescent boy, Victor, went to an "out-of-town game" after school without telling his parents. His mother talked to him after he returned that evening.

Mother: "Victor, I was concerned because I didn't know where you were, until I called your friend, Peter, who said you went to a ball game with the team."

Victor: "But I told Peter to tell you."

Mother: "Did you ask Peter to call me?"

Victor: "No, I thought you would call Peter, and then he would tell you."

Mother: "I believe this is your business, not Peter's. You're responsible for letting me or Dad

Know where you are going after school if you're not coming home."

Victor: "I know, Mom." He paused. "I'm sorry! I should have called you when I got there, but the game was too exciting. And being with the team was so fun! I'm sorry, I was wrong."

Mother: "I understand. I just want you remember, there are many things in life that will keep you busy or distract your attention, yet we have to remember our responsibilities and priorities."

Victor: "Okay, Mom."

Victor's mother used "I" and "we" messages in her communication. These were nonjudgmental and effective messages. Her purpose was to teach him to be responsible. At the same time, she gave Victor the opportunity to understand and express his mistake. The "I" message approach engages the awareness of the listener and may help the listener to acknowledge or explain the situation.

Communicating to a teenage child may be the most difficult task for some parents. I hope after reading this chapter; you have a better understanding about teens' developmental issues and needs. As parents and adults, we should be glad that our children are approaching adulthood.

Chapter 5
Communicating Effectively
with Your Spouse or Partner

Spousal or partner relationships are very special, and they are quite different from parent/child relationships or sibling relationships. In the last three chapters, our focus was on communication between parents and children at different stages. As parents, you are responsible for your children's lives—you provide for their needs and bring them up into adulthood. The relationship with your spouse is different. You and your spouse each grew up in different households. And both of you are adults, *with your own choices and beliefs.* When you became partners to each other; you chose to form a new family. Because each of you comes from a different family background, your *life experiences and expectations are also different.* At the beginning of the relationship, you may appreciate each other's differences, but as time passes your interest in the differences may gradually fade away. For instance, I heard a European wife say that when she first married, her husband liked her European accent and said, "It's cute". Now he complains about her accent.

Effective communication is a tool that spouses can use to understand each other, to express feelings and to exchange information. Both verbal and nonverbal communications are important in a couple's relationship. Most unhappy marriages are due, at least in part, to a lack of effective communication. Nevertheless, communication skills can be learned and improved.

This   chapter   is   focused   on   effectively communicating with your partner or spouse. It covers the following:

- Verbal communication
- Nonverbal communication
- Active listening
- Uncommunicative Spouse
- Communication for establishing a "couple identity"
- Resolving conflict
- Negotiation
- Controlling
- Post-parental stage

VERBAL COMMUNICATION

A verbal expression is a clear message that both the listener and the speaker can hear. It is a basic communication that spouses exchange to initiate their relationship and to continue developing their ongoing relationship. In fact, during the marriage ceremony the couple speaks their vows to each other in front of an official to signify their commitment. This is a form of verbal communication. This reminds me of a story I heard about a couple, Ellen and Andy. Andy lost his wife two years before meeting Ellen. After several months of dating, they went to Las Vegas to get married, but Andy could not bring himself to say his vows, and did not bring the wedding ring, so Ellen was upset and cancelled the marriage, and their relationship ended. Although this was an unfortunate story, I thought the breakup could have been avoided if Andy and Ellen had communicated better and understand each other better.

When two people are interested in each other, they communicate that feeling to each other. With verbal communication, the speaker *not only expresses feelings to the listener but also is able to clarify the* listener's feelings *by his or her response*. Verbal communication helps each to *exchange information*, thus *enhancing understanding*. Without communication, two people would not be able to initiate a meaningful relationship.

Starting with *appreciative, reciprocal communication as a foundation*, the couple continues to learn from each other. As they get to know each other more, each spouse even understands a particular meaning for certain words. Unlike your children who learned their first word in your family, your spouse learned basic communication *from her/his family*. Therefore, you need to allow time to get to know each other through open communication.

Example: Phil, a 30-year-old university teaching assistant, was in China participating in a research study. While he was there he met a young woman, Min-min, and they had been married for about a year before returning to the United States. Phil continued his job at the university, but eventually accepted a faculty position at a different university. The couple rented an apartment in the college town. One Friday Phil brought back a new ice chest during his lunch break. He asked his wife to wash the new ice chest in preparation for going out for the weekend. Min-min was happy and, following her husband's instructions, was about to wash the ice chest. She noticed that the picture stuck on the side of the ice chest was beautiful. It was a scene with flowers and farm animals. She liked it, and felt she would like to put it on her kitchen wall, so she pasted it on the wall with glue. She was happy, enjoying the picture. When Phil returned from work, he was astonished to see the picture label on the kitchen wall! He was upset and angry because they were living in an apartment, and the contract stated the tenant could not damage the wall by putting in nails or hanging pictures. Phil was planning to move out before September. He was upset by the thought of the cost and effort to repaint the wall. He was in a panic, just to think about it. He was *speechless!* Min-min did not know why her husband was so mad, so she was frightened, and crying. Finally, Phil explained to her that they would have to pay for all the damages. Min-min said to her husband, "You told me the kitchen is my territory and that I can do anything I want to." Phil admitted, "That was true, I said that, but…" He went on to explain the apartment lease and the regulations. This couple has had a good relationship; they were able to open up to each other, even when they have cultural differences. With a little coaching in communication, Phil and Min-min were able pinpoint their problems and improve their communication.

NONVERBAL COMMUNICATION

Nonverbal communication between spouses is often significant. From the beginning of a relationship, couples initiate their interaction with eye contact, which is a "nonverbal" message. Eye contact can be important in a relationship, because it often implies certain mutually understood messages. The most widely recognized ones are "wink" and "stare". They both indicate the feelings of the sender. These nonverbal messages attract the attention of the other party, and are as effective as verbal ones. A pat on your spouse's shoulder or touching each other are affectionate expressions. Smiling and laughing are other expressions of feelings. All of these are positive feelings. In contrast, wrinkling your forehead or tightening your eyebrows indicates a feeling of stress. When a couple lives together, they gradually learn each other's nonverbal communication. During the earlier stages of life together, the partners may not be used to decoding each other's nonverbal messages, and often become curious or even feel anxious, wondering what is going on with their partner. Some couples need more time to adjust to each other's communication patterns, especially with nonverbal messages. This is even more important in cross-cultural relationships.

Example: Marian and Hank had been married for 8 months. They were certain that they loved each other, but recently Marian had felt that Hank was quieter. He often tightened his eyebrows and seemed to be thinking. When Marian asked him what was wrong, he would not say anything. He just threw his arm*s* around her and hugged her and kissed her. Marian became puzzled and worried. One day, Marian begged him to tell her what was on his mind. Finally, Hank revealed that he was being assigned to a job overseas. If he did not take it, he would have to resign. He felt bad about leaving his wife alone at home, but he did not want to change jobs either. The worst part of it for him was that he *did not have the courage* to tell his wife, because he believed that would disrupt their newly established married life.

This example indicates that Marian *sensed* something bothering Hank. Even though he had not opened up, she thought his attitude toward her was still sweet and his nonverbal messages of hugging and kissing indicated he still loved and cared for her. With Marian's insistence, Hank shared the decision he was facing. Marian understood completely, and Hank and Marian discussed the issues together. They decided that Hank would accept the job overseas. Marian was supportive as they talked more about the job.

Hank and Marian were able to share each other's concerns because they were in a good relationship. Initially, Hank did not want to share his worries with Marian because he loved her and did not want to disappoint her, but Marian's awareness broke Hank's silence and together they worked on the issue.

ACTIVE LISTENING

The relationship between partners should be equal and reciprocal: therefore, if one person is talking, the other should be actively listening. How can you be an active listener? An active listener needs to pay attention to the message the other person is communicating. Is the message verbal or nonverbal? Regardless of whether it is verbal or nonverbal, *as an active listener you have to respond* to the message. For instance, if your spouse is talking to you and you are changing your crying baby's diaper, and you cannot hear what he is saying, your response can be, "I cannot hear you, please tell me later." This woman was an active listener, because she responded to her husband's message—his need to talk to her—even though she couldn't stop and listen right at that moment. Sometime you may feel it's too much trouble to respond every time; nevertheless, this is one of the most common complaints we hear during marital/relationship counseling sessions because many spouses *react to a non-response (inactive listening)* with,

"He/she *ignores* me". An active listener may *share honest feelings.* If you don't understand what your partner's message means, *your responding helps to clarify* so that you can understand. *Couple relationships are strengthened by effective communication and quality interaction* between the spouses.

If your partner's message is nonverbal, you still need to an actively listen and respond, but with consideration of an *appropriate manner and time.* Here is an example.

Example: It was the end of the year; Bernie had worked overtime for a whole week. Her fifty- minute drive back home was hectic and tiring. When she got in the door, Ben, her husband, met her with a warm smile on his face and wanted to give Bernie a hug. Bernie was not in the mood to respond to Ben's affection. Without a word, she kicked her shoes off and zoomed into the bedroom and lay down on her bed. After a while, she thought to herself that her attitude toward her husband had been unreasonable. She felt embarrassed, and she went to talk to her husband. She apologized for her behavior and admitted that she was in a bad mood because of the pressure from work.

Bernie's nonverbal message obviously indicated that she was unhappy, but without the follow-up verbal expression, Ben would not understand why she responded the way she did. Bernie was an open-minded person, aware of her behavior and feelings. She apologized to Ben without further damaging the relationship. In order for couples to improve their communication, both spouses need to work toward the goal of improvement. Successful communication is a vital part of a couple's relationship. Communication is always worth improving, because the marital relationship is based on how well the partners can communicate.

Sometimes statement can be puzzling and hard to understand if they are *inconsistent,* or carry a *double message,* particularly if the verbal and nonverbal communications have conflicting meanings. Here is an example:

Example: Margaret planned to go out with her friend. She told her husband, Troy, and he agreed. But when she was about to leave, Troy appeared to be upset, with a frown on his face and a clenched jaw, but he said, "Go, and go ahead! Have a good time!" Troy's verbal and nonverbal messages are inconsistent. Margaret had an uncomfortable feeling. Then, she remembered her counselor had said, "You cannot change others, but only yourself." Then she left. The fact was clear; Troy was not happy about Margaret's going out, yet he is not open enough to say what his real feeling is. Margaret cannot help him, but upon returning that night, Margaret and Troy had good communication. Margaret sincerely told Troy that if he didn't like her to go, he could let her know, and she wouldn't plan the outing. The couple's communication is based on *openness and sincerity. Inconsistent or double* messages may confuse the listener and eventually ruin a healthy relationship.

UNCOMMUNICABLE SPOUSE

There may be many reasons why your partner can't communicate.

1. Lack of verbal skills to express feelings or thoughts. Every person has different talents; some people have better verbal skills than others. Starting from the premarital stage, couples need to *openly communicate their thoughts and feelings to each other.* This communication acknowledges each person's confidence in developing sufficient love and care for each other. This way, the couple establishes communication patterns that enable them to understand and accept each other for their entire marriage. Once, at a family party, I heard a wife laugh and say to her friend about her husband, "Oh, that's the way he talks...." After 40 years of marriage, she knows her husband's communication patterns and the two of them understand and comfortably accept each other.

2. Not assertive enough to share the inner self with the spouse. If the couple did not start with open communication and were not certain about each other's feelings, it is difficult to share the inner self, because of a lack self-confidence.

3. Lack of confidence or trust in the partner. Sometime a

person withholds or refuses to share information because he is not certain how the other will react. Or, if the partner has had negative experiences related to sharing information, she will not want face another bad experience. Communication is based on the level of trust the couple has with each other. For instance, in the previous example of Marian and Hank, Hank withheld the information about his overseas assignment because he was not sure (or had a lack of trust) about what his wife Marian's reaction would be if he shared the problem.

4. Refusal to communicate may come from a spouse's negative feelings, such as anger, toward the other spouse. In this kind of situation the couple is engaged in a "cold war." It is a sad situation, and denotes an unhealthy interaction between the spouses. Besides, *it does not resolve the couple's conflicts.* When a person holds their anger inside and refuses to talk, it may be a learned communication pattern from the family they grew up in. As we discussed in the previous chapters, we learned many things from our families, and we watched our parents' interactions to each other as a couple—their communications, conflict resolution (or lack of it), etc. All these observations may influence our communication patterns in our relationships.

Sometimes one spouse is angry with the other spouse, and wants to punish the spouse by giving him/her the "cold shoulder", another common complaint in counseling sessions. This "cold war" can be ended by *negotiation*. However, to start the negotiation the couple has to have the basic feelings of love and caring for each other. *The negotiation is communication*. You can initiate the communication by talking about your spouse's favorite subjects: movies, music, sports or friends, etc.

Talk in a peaceful manner and tone, and keep the communications flowing. Then, if there is slowly a response from your partner, make eye contact with him/her, and engage in more normal discussion. You have to remember that your spouse was angry and did not want to communicate. Now that you have successfully opened the door for communication, you still may or may not know the cause of your spouse's anger. Once you have reestablished communication on a more peaceful level, you can try to resolve the issue if you choose. In order to create a better relationship in the future, you can *change this unhealthy communication pattern*. These are the some ideas to consider when you talk to your spouse:

a. Be aware that "no talk" damages the relationship.

b. Communication can be relearned and improved.

c. You both can be happy in the marriage together for the rest of your life—*only if both parties are willing to improve.*

COMMUNICATION FOR ESTABLISHING A "COUPLE IDENTITY"

Your relationship began with two individuals who were strangers to each other, and eventually become closer. Communication in a relationship is an *ongoing process*. First, it helps you to develop feelings and a commitment to each other, and then it helps to build a unique relationship *that identifies you as a couple. This is known as a "couple identity."* Couple identity *establishes a boundary that connects both partners*— they become one unit. Their parents, friends and society accept them as a couple, and their identity has changed from two single people to a married couple. After marriage, both spouses are challenged to create and improve their communication abilities. Because married life is a new experience for both spouses, they need to effectively communicate with each other— sharing each other's concerns and needs, understanding each other's differences, and communicating these differences effectively. The improvement of their communication has to be dynamic enough to keep up with each individual's growth. For instance, the husband may need to remember that his wife was an only child in her family, and in contrast, he is from a big family and was one of ten children. They both need to adjust to each other's differences, and to help each other to understand and learn from each other. Successful communication is a vital tool in connecting spouses and minimizing the gap between them.

Following the establishment of the couple identity, the couple may expect a new family member's arrival when their first child joins the household. Then the couple becomes parents, and along with the partner role to each other, they have to fulfill a parental role. The communication pattern changes according to the changes in the household. For instance, each spouse may have different expectations and philosophies regarding childrearing, and each spouse has to be able to listen to and express those differences to each other. However, this is not an easy task, so the couple may argue intensely about their different opinions regarding childrearing. They both need effective communication skills to express their own viewpoints and listen to each other's.

Successful communication is not a synonym for agreement. Your ability to *exchange your thoughts and feelings clearly* with your spouse does not imply your agreement. After the arrival of the first child, the household will become more complicated, and the couple's communication patterns need to adapt to meet the change of pace and needs of each spouse. There may be stress from a job outside the house and also from household tasks. Successful communication helps *each person release stress*, and supports each partner *by acknowledging both parties' contributions to the newly formed nuclear family.* An obvious example is that when the husband is working hard to support the family and the wife is taking care of the baby, she probably needs to provide night feeding, etc. In fact, both spouses are equally valuable in childrearing. The current trend is that many couples are both working, and send their children to daycare during the day and pick them up after work. So both spouses share the household chores and childcare. The couple needs to communicate clearly about each partner's jobs and responsibilities, so there will not be any confusion or negligence. Effective communication is an excellent tool for new parents to use to share their feelings and to express their appreciation to each other.

Example: Stan, a 27-year-old accountant, is married to Jan, who is also 27. They knew each other in college and dated for about two years. After graduation they decided to marry. They both worked until they had their first baby a year ago, when Jan quit her job to stay home and take care of their child. Both Stan and Jan have noticed that their life pattern has changed. They both love their child and they still love each other, but they often get into arguments, without any obvious reason. They sometimes even forget what they are arguing about. One day they were sharing this problem with one of their friends who is an experienced mother. She pointed out that Stan and Jan have become stressed out without realizing it. She suggested that Jan was not used to staying home, and that taking care of a first child demands a lot of attention and learning. And because Jan is not working, Stan has tried to work more overtime to make up for Jan's lost income. After their friend pointed this out, Jan and Stan became more aware of the situation. Jan noticed that because she is staying home alone with baby, she misses talking to people who can respond to her. She also realized that she waits eagerly for Stan to come home, but Stan is often late because he has been working overtime. When he does get home, he is too tired to do anything. Without them realizing it, the couple's time together has been slipping away. Their friend offered to baby-sit for them on Saturday, so they could go out together and have a good time. On that evening out, they realized how much they have been preoccupied with the new baby's arrival and care, and they were able to share their feelings and thoughts with each other. They discussed how they could readjust their life to accommodate these changes. They were surprised by how clearly they could see their problem when they took time for open communication with each other.

They thanked their friend, who had good advice because she had experienced the "young couple" journey herself.

In the above example, Stan and Jan had a strong foundation of love and care for each other. Therefore, it was easy for them to open up to each other and to be ready to accept the challenge of change. There are many young couples who lack experience, awareness, and a strong foundation of love, and cannot deal with adapting to a couple identity or to a new parental role. However, if the partners are effective communicators, they will have a better chance of sharing their feelings with each other, and sharing their problems with close friends or relatives who may help resolve the problems.

RESOLVING CONFLICT

Conflict is inevitable in human relationships, even when you try to avoid it. Because marriage involves an intimate relationship, conflict between spouses is common. What's most important in dealing with conflict is *how you look at the conflict*—i.e., *your attitude* toward the conflict. With a positive attitude, you can resolve the conflict.

Generally speaking, a relationship begins with a certain degree of mutual interest or love, and as time goes on, some conflict arises. *Conflict does not have to mean "hostility."* Conflict is almost always the result of misunderstanding or differing points of view. I have observed how couples approach their conflicts. There are three common ways, and the third is a better approach that I highly recommend. Matthew McKay, the author of the "Messages"(1995) described them as:

—*The hardheaded approach*: One spouse just wants *to win at all costs,* disregarding anybody's suggestions. The goal of this spouse is *to have his/her way and nothing less.* This spouse may apply different kinds of pressure to the other spouse in order to "win." In one interesting case, the husband had a hardheaded-approach, and had to win every conflict between himself and his wife. When they had a conflict, he insisted he was right and that his wife was definitely wrong. He put a lot of pressure on his wife, including not talking, not answering, and giving her "the angry face" (a very strong nonverbal message). But when they were in their counseling session, he actually forgot what he was angry about! Where was the conflict? Not surprisingly, his wife remembered, and she described how the conflict started. It was a small issue—the wife forgot to drop off some mail that was not in any way urgent, and the mailman would pick it up the next day anyway. But the husband was upset and complained that his wife was not paying attention. Of course this couple had many more unresolved issues in their marital relationship that I'm not covering in our discussion here.

The hardheaded approach *may result in a short-term win, but it does not create a healthy spousal relationship.* In the case above, the husband did not even remember what the real conflict was. So his win was an empty one, because it did not gain him a better relationship with his wife.

—*The softhearted approach*: This approach is just the *opposite* of the hardheaded approach. The intention of the spouse *is to reach agreement at all costs.* You follow your spouse's lead and allow him or her to take over, to win all the time. Even when it hurts your feelings or knocks down your self-esteem, you bear with it, because you just want to have "peace." I have seen this kind of attitude in married couples. Some of these cases are due to the couples' cultural backgrounds or religious beliefs. They were *taught to take this "softhearted" approach*, and they are willing to remain in this attitude. Some people of Eastern religions believe in karma, and they don't think there is a way to change that "karma." Nevertheless, in spite of "karma," taking or trying different approaches can change the relationship.

I met a beautiful young woman, Bam, who was 25 years old. She followed the traditional Asian culture and married her husband through her parents' arrangement. Her husband was a businessman. The parents arranged the marriage based on the family background and status. The young couple had one chance to see each other, but there was no further courtship or dating. Bam's parents and relatives thought Bam was fortunate to marry into a rich family. However, Bam was sad, because she knew there was no chance for her to express her opinion. She believed it was her "karma," and she just had to follow it. When they were married, her husband stayed home with her for two months, and after that he hardly spent anytime with her. She did not have a chance to talk to him or get to know him. But Bam believed that she was paying a debt *she had owed in* a *previous life, so her attitude was set. She accepted that "karma".*

—*The principled approach*: The principled approach falls between the "hardheaded" and "softhearted" approaches. The purpose of the principled approach is to focus on the principles of individual needs, to be fair to each other, to openly bring out the issues, to listen to each other and to reach a mutual agreement by open communication. The principled approach establishes mutual trust and appreciation of each other. With these principles in mind, the partners agree on a trial period to learn the principled approach. Then at the end of the trial period, they may evaluate this approach for themselves.

The principled approach takes more time and effort, but it is much more effective than hardheaded or softhearted approaches. It may require slowing down, and discarding habitual patterns. This approach is centered on open communication, and although it takes a longer time, it is healthier. If both spouses value their marriage, this is by far the best method.

Example: Howard, a 49-year-old engineer, had been married once before, and this was his second marriage. He thought this wife, Jackie, would be easier for him to relate to than his first wife. And for the first few years, their married life was quite peaceful. After their first child was born, Jackie became irritable, and Howard felt it was hard to please her. Howard said, "I am walking on eggshells every day. I have to be very careful what I say. Whatever I say, I will be wrong and she is always right." Howard continued, "I don't want to divorce again. My son is only three and he needs her. So I avoid Jackie by working late."

Howard was having a hard time resolving the conflict with his wife. According to his statement, Jackie claimed that *she was always right and Howard was wrong*. It sounds like Jackie is taking *the "hardheaded approach"—she wanted to win all the time*. And Howard did not know what to do. My evaluation of this case was that Howard did not have a clear understanding of the marriage relationship. He could not take any position to resolve the conflict, and he was continually suffering. I helped Howard to re-examine his *attitude toward marriage*. After a long discussion, Howard realized he did not have specific expectations or goals in his marriage; he just wanted to marry and have a peaceful, easier life for himself. Howard said, "I am tired of fighting. When I was young I saw enough of my parents' fights. Now I am doing the same thing." Howard continued, "I just want to have a peaceful life. I love Jackie and our son." During an individual session with Jackie, I discovered that Jackie really cared for Howard. They enjoyed each other's company. They had a good time together, but after their first child, they started to neglect each other. She had been busier with work and childcare, and Howard worked more and came home late. Jackie cried and said, "I am tired of waiting for him. He doesn't understand—I need him to be with me." She sounded so sad, but Howard didn't understand her needs, *because she didn't tell him*. They were not communicating their needs to each other.

After I listened to both Howard and Jackie, I knew

they loved each other. They had a good bond, but they didn't know how to resolve their conflict. They needed to learn the "principled approach" to resolve their conflict, so in the joint session, I encouraged Jackie to let Howard know that she was lonely and needed his company (this is *her need*). Howard was surprised, and softly mentioned that her agitated mood scared him away. He wanted to have a peaceful home (and this is *his need*). He said, "I love you and our son." In order to open the communication, they shared their needs, even though it was uncomfortable: Jackie wanted her husband's company and Howard wanted a nice and peaceful home. Their needs are not contradictory and the problem was not complicated, but they did not openly communicate with each other and share their needs and feelings.

The examples above indicate the importance of effective communication between partners. Because everyone is different, without open communication they cannot understand each other. The more they communicate, the more they get to know each other. Therefore, the first few years are the most important time for couples to openly communicate and to adjust to each other. This is especially true after the birth of their first child.

NEGOTIATION

Negotiation is closely related to the topic we have just discussed, "resolving conflict." *Negotiation is a way of resolving conflict.* Negotiation is a helpful interpersonal skill. In a partnership when two people are living together, in many ways they are very close—both physically and emotionally. I have listened to a couple argue about how to share their blanket at night, because one preferred a heavier blanket and the other preferred a lighter one. It sounds like a small matter, but if one partner felt he/she was taken advantage of or was sacrificing for the other partner, it would hurt their relationship in the long run. Every couple has differences, but *regardless of the differences or opposition* between them, there must be *compatible interests.* Negotiation starts from *being aware of those compatible interests and communicating* to the partner or spouse about those interests. Some common compatible interests for couples include the following: we were madly in love, we have cared for each other, we both love music, etc. When you talk to your spouse or partner about your compatible interests, you sense the empathetic feelings in each other, and *the common bond of the interests will bring you closer to each other again,* even when there are conflicts or disagreements. However, when you find your spouse in a bad mood or a disagreeable state, you may feel like staying away from your spouse, just like Howard did in the previous example. He *avoided* his wife by working late, but didn't resolve the conflict. Instead, it worsened the relationship.

Howard and Jackie learned a new approach to resolve the conflict, which is one form of negotiation.

For another couple, the conflict was over the blanket—heavier versus lighter. The negotiation seems like it should have been easy: use two blankets separately in the same bed, so each can use whichever they prefer. It sounds simple. But it's not that simple— underneath most couples' conflicts there are uncovered or unresolved issues, such as suppressed anger and complaints that are not revealed. All those are tucked undercover, or under the blanket—and they fight. As I see it, many of these uncovered or unresolved issues are control and power issues, which are covered in the next discussion.

CONTROLLING

Some spouses or partners give the other spouse the impression that they are the controlling or dominant spouse, because of the way they communicate. Some of them truly are controlling, and some of them just seem that way because of their communication style. In Chapter One, "Key Concepts in Effective Communication," I explained the different "ego states" from which people communicate. If someone talks to his or her partner from the *parent ego state* most of the time, the listening partner will feel that he/she is controlled by the talker. If they understand each other and accommodate well to each other, the relationship may not be jeopardized. Nevertheless, using the parental ego state to communicate with your partner is not effective in creating healthy communication, because you may be perceived as an authoritarian or a dominant person. A good couple relationship is based on mutual respect and reciprocal intimacy, with both parties nurturing each other and enjoying their life together. However, sometimes a partner is not aware of their communication pattern, and hurts their partner's feelings without intending to. Here is an example:

Example: Paul, a 35-year-old entrepreneur, was an only son and was well provided for and well educated. He worked hard and smoothly reached his business goals. He married his high school sweetheart, Lilly. They have enjoyed their marriage for 7 years, and they have three children. Life seemed great for this couple. But recently, Lilly has been complaining of headaches and being tired. Her doctor didn't find any physical problems. Paul thought that she was just tired and that she needed more help around the house. So Paul hired a live-in housekeeper to manage the housework. But Lilly's condition did not improve. Finally, with the recommendation of their family doctor, they came to see a marriage counselor. The counselor helped them to see that they had poor communication. Lilly was not happy about their relationship, but didn't know exactly how to express that, because Paul was nice to her and cared for her. But he had been the "leader" in the marriage, making all the decisions for her to follow. Lilly had lost interest in this marriage; she was tired of following her husband's orders. Paul could not understand what he had done wrong. It seemed to him that he worked hard and took care of his family, and he loved his wife. Their therapist gave the couple an assignment. They had to put a tape recorder on the top of the piano in the living room for a week, and bring it back to the next session. When the therapist and the couple listened together to the recorded tape, the therapist pointed out to Paul that his communications were mostly in the parental ego state, such as, "You should not open that window," "You call him again today, don't forget!" and "You need to go to the bank soon." As Lilly said, she was tired of listening to and following orders. Until he heard the tape and the therapist's comments about it, Paul did not recognize his authoritarian pattern of communication. He was used to being in control because he was brought up as an only child in his family and had his own business.

In contrast, Lilly was a rather quiet person, used to taking care of people without complaint. Both parties in a marriage need mutual respect and nurturing. As the years passed, and Lilly compared her own life to her husband's exciting business life, she felt tired and bored. She had a "good" husband, but she didn't know how to express her unhappiness, and therefore she had headaches.

Now both Paul and Lilly have learned a new way to communicate with each other. Lilly can tell Paul what she likes and dislikes. Paul has learned to communicate more from the adult ego state. He respects Lilly's abilities and interests, and fully supports her ideas. At the last joint session Lilly said to the therapist, "I feel now I am happily married. Paul is a nice person!" And Paul echoed, "I am happy too. We are a lucky couple."

POST-PARENTAL STAGE

"Empty-nest syndrome" is a well-known life transition. After children leave for college, or move out to live elsewhere, the house seems quiet, with too much empty space. The couple may lose topics of conversation and common ground for their communications—no ball games to talk about, no sleepover parties to plan. Wives and mothers may have spent a lot of time and energy bringing up the children.

Now the couple may have nothing to talk about. For 18 years or more, the couple has been connected to each other through their children, regardless of how much each spouse has been involved in taking care of them. Without awareness and preparation before the last child leaves home, a couple can have a hard time adjusting to this life transition.

Example: Roy and Christina have been married for twenty years. Last year, their first son left for college, and this year their second son, Peter left for college as well. Roy was glad that he and his wife successfully launched their boys. He had felt that all these years Christina was busy with two boys and that he had been somewhat neglected, but he could not complain. Now he thought it should be his turn, and he wanted to spend some quality time with his wife. But Christina missed her children. Especially after Peter left, she felt empty and lonely. She kept in touch with her sons by e-mail and phoned them almost every day. Roy was disappointed, because Christina's life was still centered on the children. The boys also needed some independence, and said, "Mom, we are okay at school. We have many new friends and a lot to learn. Besides, we have each other here. So don't worry about us."

Christina has not adjusted to this new life stage. She has been clinging to her children, an unhealthy family pattern. Finally, Christina and her husband attended a seminar on "life after launching your children." The presentation helped her to see and understand her problem. Roy also became more supportive, and initiated more activities the two of them could do together. In fact, they traveled to places that they had talked about for many years, but had never visited because their children were too young to go or their school schedules were not suitable for long travel. Christina and Roy have found many new ways to share time together. They walk together in the park, and go to movies, almost as if they are re-experiencing the time they were dating. This helps them build a new foundation in their relationship for this next life stage.

There are many positive ways to enrich your life and improve your communication if you are both open-minded and willing to learn. This stage also leads into the retirement stage, and if the couple is adjusting effectively after launching their children, they are more ready to enjoy their retirement life.

Chapter 6
All in the Family

In previous chapters, we discussed how our communication skills are learned within the family system and that we continue to learn and develop our skills throughout the different stages of life. We started with the key concepts in successful communication, and then looked at how parents may communicate effectively with their children at different ages. Following the outline of concepts for communicating with your children, then, the discussion centered on effective communication with your significant person—spouse or partner. All of these types of communication take place primarily between two parties: between parent and children, or between spouses / partners.

This chapter covers a different type of communication in family settings, which is not limited to one person talking and the other listening. It can be more than one person talking or more than one listening, and other family members may interject comments into the conversation. This is common in a family setting. For instance, when a mother is talking to her daughter about chores, the grandmother may make comments. The grandmother's comments may be a positive or negative influence on the mother/daughter communication. Nevertheless, we love our families and most of us enjoy family gatherings. Almost every family has family gatherings, such as holidays or reunions. You enjoy talking and listening to your relatives—they may be cousins whom you used to play with, or your uncle who remembers your grandparents' stories. While listening and talking to family members and relatives may provide warm and joyful moments to many people, to some these may be unbearable moments.

A young woman in her late twenties told me she felt tortured by many of her relatives' comments at her grandmother's birthday party. She knew that it would happen, but she missed her relatives so she went anyway. I will discuss this young woman's situation in detail later in this chapter. Although we love our families and relatives, the communication in family settings may not always be a pleasant experience. However, that unpleasantness can be minimized or avoided with effective communication skills. The following are the topics covered in this chapter that are important to communication within the family system

- Covert messages
- Triangulation
- Deletion
- Domination and Control

- Ambivalent messages
- Denial
- Mind Reading
- Blended family

COVERT MESSAGES

All communication has an implied meaning. Even a simple greeting like "good morning" has its purpose. We talk or listen in order to communicate, and we often want to influence the other party. But sometimes a person does not directly or openly express the real purpose of his/her words, and the real meaning is hidden underneath—we call this *a hidden agenda* or *a covert message*. Here is an example of a covert message. A teenager wanted to go out. He went to his mother and said, "Mom, would you like me to put some gas in your car? I noticed it was kind of low. If I go out now to fill the tank, you won't be rushed tomorrow." Mother: "That's all right, I don't have work tomorrow. But tell me, is your real purpose to use my car to go out tonight?" Her son was a little embarrassed, but admitted he did want to use the car.

There are many reasons for communicating in covert messages:

1. Fear of rejection: The speaker is uncertain about the outcome. The conversation between the teenager and his mother above is an example. The son was not sure about his mother's response; therefore he covered up his real reason. But his mother knew his hidden agenda, and provided an effective intervention.

2. Lack of understanding: Not enough knowledge to present the facts. In these cases, it seems easier to cover up, or to be vague. Here is an example: A father and

mother and their adult son were sitting in the living room talking. The mother asked, "I wonder when that bridge work will be completed?" The father answered, "Oh, I don't know. Don't ask me." Then the mother said, "Jimmy, would you know? You have friends working in the highway department." Jimmy said, "Well, let me see, they said.... it will take a couple more months." Jimmy's answer was vague, because he did not know, but he wanted to give his mother an answer.

3. A need to block the information. Sometimes a speaker purposely blocks out information, so the communication becomes a covert message. This communication pattern can be either healthy or unhealthy, depending on the purpose of the speaker. If the purpose of holding information back is to benefit the interpersonal relationship, it contributes to healthy

communication. A good example is when we block out "gossip" we heard, not passing it on. This is blocking the message, yet it is a nice thing to do. However, blocking information for the purpose of benefiting the speaker or jeopardizing the relationship with others is an unhealthy communication.

Example: Lynn and her mother in-law, Louise, are not close. Louise is a 63-year-old widow. According to Lynn, Louise is physically healthy and capable, but emotionally she clings excessively to her children, especially to her oldest son, Mark—Lynn's husband. Mark has a younger brother and a younger sister, who are not married. Usually Louise calls Mark around six o'clock every day. Recently, Mark had to work late, so when Louise called, Mark was not home. Lynn purposely did not tell Louise in advance that Mark would be late. According to Lynn, she wanted to train her mother-in-law to be independent, because Lynn dislikes Louise's always clinging to Mark. Lynn's intention to help Louise become independent sounded like a good idea; however, she did not handle it properly. Instead, Lynn blocked the information. Blocking information may entangle family relationships and may cause family disturbances. The next day, Louise was very upset and almost hysterical. Mark was also upset and blamed Lynn for having an uncaring attitude toward his mother. They had a serious family meeting with Mark's brother and sister also present. I was invited to participate and provide advice. My intervention at the family meeting helped them to realize that Louise needs love and care from her family. She also needs support to be "self-sufficient", which will increase her confidence and will make everyone around her happy and relieved. Lynn was glad to hear my suggestion, and she apologized to her mother-in-law.

AMBIVALENT MESSAGES ARE CAUSED BY AN INTERNAL CONTRADICTION

Ambivalence in human communication is common, because people often have contradicting thoughts or feelings within themselves without realizing it. When family communications are ambivalent, they create confusion and stress, because contradictory messages make a listener confused and frustrated. We lose direction in trying to follow the messages. There are many clinical studies indicating that ambivalent communication affects people's mental health, creates confusion in people's thinking, and hurts their feelings. How exactly does "ambivalent communication" operate in a family setting? Here is an example:

Example: Bruce and Joan appear to be a lovely couple. They have been married for fifteen years. According to Bruce, Joan often initiates arguments, and complains without reason or warning. Bruce says that *Joan can be very sweet and lovely, and she also can act very ugly and mean.* Sometimes, Bruce wonders how two such opposite messages can come out of the same mouth. I asked Bruce to give an illustration. Bruce said that Joan told him he was a thoughtful husband, and she felt lucky to be his wife. Then, the next day Joan was mad at him for a whole night because he forgot to pick up the shirts at the dry cleaner. Actually, the shirts were not that urgently needed, and Bruce thought Joan's blow-up was out of proportion. He could not understand how could she praise him one day and punish him the next. This situation had happened on and off for fifteen years. Bruce loved Joan, but he often felt frustrated and confused about what she really meant. After a big argument, he suggested they seek help. During the individual sessions, Joan shared her family background. Joan had had an unhappy childhood. She lost her father when she was four, and her mother worked to support three children. Since Joan was the oldest, sometimes she had to go live with her grandmother in order to lighten her mother's load. She did not have a stable home environment. She said she is happier now with Bruce, but she was not aware of how she had been hurting Bruce.

Most of the time, Joan was not aware of her ambivalent communication. My assignment was for Bruce to help her, *to make her aware of her pattern in a nice way, not in an angry way*. Bruce used to argue back strongly because he was *frustrated by her contradictory behavior*. Then their argument would escalate, and oftentimes Bruce would slam the door and leave the house. Now they have to *learn a new pattern,* which is not easy, but they care about their marriage and they don't want their children, ages 12 and 9, to continue this pattern. Since Joan was not aware of the internal strain which resulted in her giving contradictory messages, I told Bruce to point out to Joan every time her message was ambivalent, and asked her to clarify her *real feeling or thought.* Fortunately, Bruce was a supportive husband, and Joan's individual sessions also helped her recover from her unhealthy childhood experience. Joan has paid more attention to her communication pattern, and the couple's relationship has improved.

TRIANGULATION

A family setting can consist of two people or more than two. When two people interact calmly and their communication indicates their appreciation of each other, their situation is stable. However, *when the connection between them becomes uncomfortable and unstable* and tension builds up between them, the system will quickly draw in another, *vulnerable person to make a triangle*, in order to stabilize the system. People are usually not even aware that they are doing this. When tension in the triangle is too great for the three to handle, it will pull others in to become a *series of interlocking triangles*. And remember, communication is involved in all these interactions in triangles. Sometime the triangulation is not limited to family members living in the same household, but includes family members living in different places. Especially now that we have convenient communication tools like cell phones and the internet, it is easy to create a triangle. For example, a young woman who was living alone often had conflict with her mother. One day she became so upset after talking on the telephone with her mother, she made a long-distance telephone call to her sister to complain and ask for help. This is a long-distance triangle—now her sister is caught in the middle.

Family communication should connect family members in a positive, supportive way. When the communication creates tension between two people, the two who are involved have to resolve it themselves. Although good communication takes time and effort, and involving a third party by making a triangle may be a quick solution, the family misses the opportunity to learn problem-solving skills if they quickly involve another family member in the situation. The most common triangle in families consists of a father, mother and child relationship. Here are two examples:

Example 1: Cathy and her mother are very close to each other, while her father is more devoted to his work and does not have time for the family. Cathy has been good company and a good listener for her mother. Her mother tells Cathy about many of her father's faults. Cathy is grown up and married, but her mother still calls her and tells her about her father's wrongdoings, such as coming home late, drinking too much, having rowdy friends, etc. Each time her mother calls, Cathy gets upset, and this problem affects her relationship with her husband. Finally, Cathy suggested to her mother: "Mom, why don't you tell Dad your concerns about his behaviors and your feelings? I can't always be there to comfort you. I want you to be able to handle this yourself and to be happy. And it's good for Dad to know your concerns." Later Cathy suggested that her mother to see a family therapist.

Cathy's mother *involved her in a triangle, to stabilize her marital conflicts* by reducing her stress. This is a triangulation pattern that influences Cathy's relationship with her father. *After Cathy married and left home, the stabilizer (Cathy) was gone*, and then the family system lost its balance. Cathy cared about her parents' relationship, but she cannot be part of a triangle; therefore, Cathy told her mother to *communicate directly, which is a healthy pattern, called de-triangulation.*

The relationship between Cathy's mother and father improved, and Cathy still calls her mother often, but leaves the parents' relationship issue alone.

Example 2: Don, a 12-year-old boy, and his parents were eating dinner. Don's father paid a lot of attention to table manners and corrected Don's manners often. Sometime Don's father used derogatory remarks which upset Don. Don's mother, Shirley, felt sorry for her son and always came to his rescue. Shirley would blame her husband and make him stop hurting Don's feelings. Don appreciated his mother's interjections, but the mood at the dinner table was still not pleasant. When Don's mother was discussing this problem with me after a parenting workshop, my suggestions were: 1) Support and encourage Don. Let Don know that he can and needs to protect himself. Shirley may explore with Don how he could avoid and defend himself from his father's verbal abuse. 2) Shirley may support her son by discussing proper table manners with him and helping him in the areas where his father was correcting him.

Shirley communicated these points to Don, so he could be prepared before dinner. The outcome of Shirley's support was positive, and Shirley withheld herself from the triangle. The father's attitude also improved.

DENIAL

Denial in family communication can be disturbing, and affects mutual trust. When people do not want to or are afraid to express something, they tend to deny, either overtly or covertly. Examples of overt denial are, "I don't know," "I don't care," or "Maybe." Covert denials are harder to identify, because people often convey them in a monotone or in nonverbal forms such as shrugging their shoulders or withdrawing eye contact, which means, "I don't care," or "I don't want to talk." Once I knew a 12-year-old Asian girl, Mariko, who was at the stage where she avoided talking or sharing her feelings. Her father was very upset that Mariko often shrugged her shoulders when he asked her questions or talked to her. One day Mariko's father told her, "If you shrug your shoulders again instead of answering me, I'm going to put a piece of brick on each of your shoulders. See if you can shrug them again then!" Mariko was denying her father covertly. Do you think Mariko changed after her father's warning? She might not shrug her shoulders in front of her father, but she could still avoid expressing herself. Because her father did not give her opportunity to express herself, she felt uncomfortable expressing herself, so she shrugged instead. Her father's demand that she change made it even worse. You might wonder why her father didn't give her the opportunity to express. For this family I know it's the family system and cultural issues. Many cultures believe that the father has the authority and children should listen and obey without comment.

DELETION

We often notice people talking without completing a whole sentence. For example, two friends are talking: "You know James is back..." Answer: "Back from where, from New York?" "No, no, he came back from

Japan." This speaker assumes that the listener knows as much about the situation as he does. But that is not always the case. And oftentimes, the listener will try to fill the blanks to make the message complete, like this: "So James came back from New York, then left for Japan, and now he has returned from Japan?" "Yeah, that's right." If the listener did not ask the speaker a question to clarify the missing information, the communication would be confusing. Deletion may lead the listener to assume that he/she can fill in the incomplete part of the message, which may not be the "true" message of the speaker. Sometimes the deletion is not even obvious, so the listener has no way of knowing that information is missing.

Avoiding deletion in family communication is important, because it can eliminate confusion and entanglement in the family. We have a tendency to believe that the family members know each other well enough that we do not need to complete whatever message we are communicating, but that's not true. Complete expression makes for much better communication. Deletion omits important parts of communication—openness and directness. And these are closely related to the next topic, Mind Reading.

MIND READING

Mind reading involves forming a belief about what others think or feel without direct communication with that person. It is often seen in family communication— for example, in this kind of conversation between siblings: "I know mom won't let you go." "How do you know that?" "Well, because..." The speaker pauses and is silent. His belief comes from an assumption, not because he talked with their mother. Another example is forming a belief about what someone is thinking or feeling from his or her nonverbal communication, without asking what's going on.

Mind reading without a firm verification is not a healthy communication pattern in the family. It can jeopardize the relationship among family members. Because a family has more than one person, and they are often living together in a close relationship, they may have a tendency to believe they can read each other's minds. Sometimes one family member will expect others to read his or her mind because of feelings of discomfort in communicating directly. But direct, open communication is important in establishing an effective communication pattern in the family, so that everyone can share their thoughts and feelings.

Mind reading skips the valuable experience of open and a direct communication. Here is an example:

Example: Harry called his wife, Peggy, from the

office and said he would be late because he needed to train a new staff member. He told Peggy not to wait dinner for him. At dinner, Peggy told her teenage daughter, Annie, "I bet your dad went to play bridge tonight. He told me he had to train a new staff member, but I know this is Friday—bridge night—and he knows I don't like him playing bridge every Friday night, so he made an excuse for being home late." Annie: "Are you sure, mom? He may be really working at the office." Around nine o'clock, Harry came home and brought the new staff person with him to meet his family.

Peggy's assumption was wrong, and her daughter, Annie, was happy that she did not go along with her mother's *mind-reading behavior*. The next morning, Annie asked her mom: "Mom, did you tell dad about what you thought he was doing last night?" Her mother said, "I did. I was kind of embarrassed, but I told him that you had better judgment. You had trust in your dad, and he was happy."

This family was about to entangle and complicate the family relationship because of Peggy's assumption, based on her mind reading without waiting for clarification. However, this family has a basic respect for each other, and has an open communication pattern. Therefore, the family was able to keep harmony among its members.

DOMINATION AND CONTROL

In a family setting, it is usually not hard to tell who the dominant party is in the conversation, or who is in control of the communication. The dominant person may use more "I" messages, which indicate power and authority, and signify the speaker's ego state, as we discussed previously in Chapter One. Another method of dominance and control is interrupting people's comments and dominating the conversation. The interruption can be with or without overlapping of words. Here are some examples: At a family dinner, a mother is talking to her teenage son. "Dean, you have to bring the registration form to your coach tomorrow." Before Dean's mother finishes her sentence, Dean's father interrupts her words and says, "Yeah, you bring it to your coach." Dean's father was interrupting by overlapping the message. Sometimes people may interrupt other's conversations without intention or awareness. Nevertheless, the speaker who was interrupted may feel *dominated and controlled* because he/she did not have a chance to finish the sentence. Interrupting when others are talking is a poor communication pattern, and is harmful to interpersonal relationships. It is especially disturbing in close relationships, such as between spouses or partners, and between a parent and their children.

Example: Kevin and Pam invited some of their friends over. Kevin was telling them about the movie he and Pam had watched recently. Their friends were interested in the story, but Pam constantly interjected her thoughts into Kevin's story and said, "Let me tell you..." and she usually repeated the same thing Kevin had just said. After a few interruptions, Kevin became quiet and let Pam finish the movie story. That night Kevin was rather quiet, and withdrew into his reading. He was upset that Pam always interrupted when he talked, but he did not express his feelings openly to Pam. Pam was not aware that she had interrupted Kevin's conversation, but she noticed Kevin was not happy after the gathering. Pam asked Kevin what made him unhappy. Then the couple had an opportunity to open up and discuss their communication patterns. Kevin expressed that he felt dominated by Pam. Kevin said that

Pam reminded him of his mother. His mother was very controlling, so as a young boy, Kevin felt he was powerless. Whenever his mother interrupted him, he just shut his mouth and buried his head in his reading.

Pam and Kevin had an opportunity to understand each other by attending counseling sessions. In contrast to Kevin's family, Pam was brought up in a "free spirited" type of family. Pam talked and laughed at any time, anywhere, as she pleased. Thus, Pam did not realize she had interrupted Kevin's conversation. Pam has discovered the root of the problem, and she was glad to improve her communication skill and her relationship with Kevin.

BLENDED FAMILY

A blended family can produce a crisis. However, just as the Chinese character "crisis" includes two compositions—"danger and opportunity"—it can provide opportunity for the family as well as difficulty. Whether it provides difficulty or opportunity depends on *how* the family members connect and interact with each other. And the *how* is primarily *through communication*. Blended families are complicated, and so are the communications in blended families. Whether the family is blended because of death or divorce and remarriage, or another reason, the family members need extra awareness and attention in talking and listening. The following are some often-discussed issues for blended families.

1. Blended family members come with *different historical backgrounds*. The family needs to *face these differences and adjust to them*.

2. For blended families, the *family circle is expanded*.

For instance, children may have more than one set of parents and grandparents.

3. Children in blended families often find an *additional parental figure* who may effectively *supplement or complement their needs*, or conversely *may deprive them of having their needs met.*

4. Blended families may still carry a shadow of pain and loss, or other emotional or financial burdens from an earlier marriage or family situation.

5. The relationships in blended families are *new and untested*, so these families need *time* to *blend into a new family system.*

In order to resolve the above issues, *effective*

communication skills are crucial in blended families. The blended family members need to understand and share with each other by *talking and listening effectively* because the communication in this family can be *complicated and can easily create confusion.* For this reason, I included *communication in blended families* here in a separate chapter, in order to meet those special needs. The following are some issues relating to blended families:

- Intrusion versus respect of boundaries
- Avoid entangling yourself
- Avoid using children as messengers
- Understand and respect children's needs

INTRUSION VERSUS RESPECT OF BOUNDARIES

Intrusions from ex-spouses and relatives are common problems. They can be related to parenting or financial issues, but regardless of the kind of issue, you need to be an effective communicator. *People intrude on others' privacy by talking improperly* or *listening improperly, as in eavesdropping on private conversations.* In order to prevent intrusions, you have to learn how to *protect your boundaries.* The next discussions show how to do that.

AVOID ENTANGLING YOURSELF

If the speaker intends to involve you in another family member's private matters, *try to stay away by changing the subject,* or *clearly state, "I don't know,"* or *"I don't think I need to know."* Example: Pam met her ex-mother-in-law on the street one day. Her mother-in-law greeted her sweetly and said, "Pam, do you know Randy and Helen are going to adopt a girl from India? I bet they are tired of trying to have a child!" Pam listened, and treated that statement as unimportant information, and said, "Is that right? I'm on the way to an appointment. It's been nice to see you today." Pam treated her with courtesy, but avoided entanglement by protecting her boundaries. Sometimes you might be curious about the information and you want to hear more, but that can bring you into entanglement. If the relationship has been terminated, you should avoid the involvement and observe mutual respect. Besides, *one entanglement may lead to more entanglements* and *create endless headaches*. Entanglement and triangles are common in blended families with children. In order to avoid these problems you need to clearly and directly communicate with the other parties.

AVOID USING CHILDREN AS MESSENGERS

If you really need to use children as messengers, the message should be in writing, and you should make sure it has been received. An example is: "Bobby's teacher/parent conference will be at 9 a.m. on Tuesday October 12. I will meet you at school before 9 a.m. at the entrance hallway." This should be in writing and put in an envelope for Bobby to carry to his father. And later you should call him to confirm the meeting. *Children in blended families can be confused* by their parents' divorce, or from the complications between two sets of families. Protect children from entanglement, and don't involve them in parents' issues. *Help children to understand their boundaries and protect them.* Sometimes children may try to save their parent's marriage, so if you use your children to pass your messages orally to the other parent, your children may use the opportunity for their own interests. Bobby's mother was careful to avoid confusion. Bobby said to his mother, "When I visit my Dad Saturday, I will tell Dad to pick you up for the parent's conference, okay?" He was trying to recreate the intimacy his parents felt in the past. It was right for Bobby's mother to give her ex-husband the message in writing and to keep Bobby out of the arrangement.

UNDERSTAND AND RESPECT CHILDREN'S NEEDS BEFORE BLENDING THE FAMILY

Teddy was a very active 4-year-old boy. Recently his parents divorced, and his father moved to a different city to be closer to his new partner. Teddy and his mother continued to live in the same house. Teddy has been very sad about his parents' divorce, and misses his father. One day, Teddy's pre-school teacher called his mother and told his mother that Teddy had fallen on the playground. Teddy's mother rushed to school and took him to the Emergency Room. The doctor found that Teddy had broken his leg, and needed to have surgery. Teddy's father was notified; he flew back and rushed to the hospital. When Teddy woke up from anesthesia, he opened his eyes, saw his father at his bedside and said, "Daddy, you are back! I'm glad! I am tired," then Teddy went back to sleep. The next day when Teddy woke up, his mother had just left the room, but his father was with him. Teddy quickly asked, "Where is Mommy?" His father explained that his mother would be back shortly. Teddy said, "I just want my Daddy and Mommy to be with me all the time, please, Daddy!" *This is a child's feeling.*

To help your children adjust to their newly blended family is not an easy task. You need to communicate with your children clearly, with an open-minded attitude, and *to listen to their feelings.* Help them to understand the parent's situation, and assure them that their parents' love and care are still there for them.

After Teddy was discharged from the hospital,

Teddy and his parents attended few sessions of family therapy. The therapy goal was to help Teddy understand that his parents were not happy with their marriage, and that divorce was their final decision. I also saw Teddy in individual play therapy. Teddy was relaxed and was able to share many of his thoughts and feelings through game-playing and drawing. Teddy said he used to be frightened when his parents argued and were mad at each other. And he used to pray to God to stop their fights. Teddy also said, "I thought I was lucky I fell and broke my leg, and brought my Dad home."

I talked to Teddy with simple language, and I used nonverbal communication as well. I assured Teddy that I would support him and help him. I gave him a big smile and patted his shoulder. Teddy agreed with my explanation that "Your parents don't want to be friends with each other any more. They'd rather be divorced and living apart, so they don't fight all the time. But they both love you very much, and wanted to be with you and take care of you. That's why you stay here with mom when you go to school, but when summer vacation comes, you go to spend summer with your dad." I helped Teddy to understand that his parents' divorce is not his responsibility, and he should not be involved. Finally, he told me that he feels better because he no longer had to watch his parents' arguments. I also had each parent join family play-therapy sessions with Teddy. I facilitated their communication during the family play-session. Teddy's parents had an opportunity to learn how to communicate to a 4-year-old child about big issues like "divorce" or "blended family." Soon Teddy would have a blended family, because Teddy's father was planning to remarry the following spring, and Teddy would have a stepmother and a stepsibling in his dad's house. When Teddy visits his dad in the summer, he will be in a blended family. All these expected events should be communicated carefully to Teddy. Teddy's parents were advised about this in advance during the parents' session, so they knew how to prepare him before visiting. Teddy's father also promised Teddy he would call him twice a week, and said that Teddy could call him whenever he misses him.

*Another example of involving the children in the blended family: When divorce and separation happen in a family, the children in the family can become confused and try in their own way to bring the family back together, just like Teddy did in the example above. However, sometimes children may create a chaotic situation that puts the blended family into an even worse situation. Ginger, a 12-year-old girl, is the only child in the family. Her parents have been divorced for a few years. She lives with her mother, Marian, who is working as a computer programmer. Marian had a boyfriend named Jackson, to whom she was engaged to be married next year. Jackson often visited Marian at her house, but Ginger never welcomed him. In fact, Ginger told her mother clearly that she wished her mother wouldn't remarry. Marian never took Ginger's words seriously, but thought that it was just a childish wish. Because Ginger was the only child in the family, she had been loved and somewhat pampered by her parents and grandparents. Ginger is very close to her mother. As Marian got involved with Jackson, Ginger began to feel she was not her mother's favorite, but that Jackson came first. Ginger told her grandmother that she hates Jackson, that she wishes

Jackson would disappear. One day, Ginger's school counselor called Marian and wanted her to come to school for a discussion. According to the school counselor, Ginger reported that she was sexually assaulted by her mother's fiancé, Jackson. By law, the school had to report this to The Child Protection Service (CPS), and the CPS would investigate the situation. Marian was shocked by the information; she could not believe Jackson would assault her daughter. On the same day, Jackson was interviewed by the investigator, and it was recommended that Ginger live with her grandmother, who lived near Marian. That way Ginger could go to the same school, and Marian could visit Ginger and take care of her needs. During the investigation, Jackson was not allowed to see Ginger. Marian was very sad—she did not realize her daughter's feelings were so intense and that she was so desperate. Marian and Jackson agreed to put their relationship on hold until the investigation was over, and then they would reevaluate their relationship, including future family plans. Jackson said he had not behaved improperly toward Ginger, but he admitted that he had not particularly cared for her or considered her as an important person relating to his fiancée. Ginger was very upset during this period, since she had to go through many interviews and evaluations. She cried a lot and exhibited symptoms of depression. Her schoolwork was affected. The investigation did not find any evidence of sexual assault, and the case was closed.

Ginger, Marian and Jackson received some individual and family therapy sessions to improve their perspective on parenting and their communication skills. The following are the major points included in their sessions:

- Accept that a blended family is an opportunity, and also a challenge.
- Be aware of your own needs as well as other's needs.
- Work on open communication—keep an open-minded attitude to listen and talk to each other.
- Enjoy each other in the blended family, and help each other share peace and harmony.

Ginger was sorry she made up the story, but she felt she *needed to do something*. She had not expected to create that much trouble. Marian admitted that it was inconsiderate on her part to make Ginger feel she was in second place. And she said she was sorry about the incident, but gained much knowledge about parenting and blended family issues. Jackson also said he should be more considerate and caring about Ginger, because if he loves Marian and wants to have a family with her, Ginger is part of the family.

This chapter covered a variety of communication issues in the family setting. These are practical issues, and we hear or experience them all the time. I hope after reading this chapter you are more aware of the nature of the problems in family communication and are more able to avoid negative experiences and create positive ones.

It is possible to communicate more successfully because we can learn new skills to augment what we learned from our family. When we become adults, we can learn new communication skills so that we can create a more peaceful, happy, and healthy family environment, and other family members will learn from our use of effective communication skills as well.

Before you started the book, you took the Pre-test, and now I recommend you take the Post-test to evaluate what you have learned. The questions on the Pre-test and Post-test are the same, and the answers follow the Post-test.

POST-TEST

1. You would like to improve your communication. Which areas do you think you need to improve?

    A. ____Talking, expressing.

    B. ____Listening.

    C. ____Both.

2. You are talking to your brother and you have a feeling that he is not listening to you, because he:

    A. _____

    B. _____

3. For the above situation, as an older sibling you feel like changing or correcting him. Which is/are your choice(s)?

    A. ____Confront him, and tell him to pay attention.

    B. ____Change the subject.

    C. ____Try to understand why your brother is not interested in talking.

    D. ____Just stop talking to him.

4. Mr. Stone is a powerful boss. His workers avoid talking to him because he acts in a condescending way towards his subordinates and that makes people uncomfortable.

Mr. Stone's communication pattern is called the:

A. ___Parental ego state

B. ___Adult ego state

C. ___Child ego state

5. If you were working for Mr. Stone, which ego state you would prefer him to use in communicating with you? Explain why.

A. ___Parental ego state

B. ___Adult ego state

C. ___Child ego state

Because:_____

6. A counselor suggested to the mother of an adolescent that the mother use "I" messages to communicate with her son, because they are more effective and more likely to motivate her son. The counselor's suggestion is based on:

A. The "I" message secures the mother's position as a "mother".

B. The "I" message shares the mother's feelings and is less demanding or criticizing.

7. To teach your child to be an effective communicator, at which stage would you start?

    A. ___You would start when the child is an infant, because communication is sharing and connection.

    B. ___You would wait until the child starts school, because school-age children are more effective in learning.

    C. ___You focus on teaching communication when the child reaches adolescence, because adolescence is a crucial stage.

8. You have a three-year-old son and you are a busy parent. You have to prioritize your time. Which would you choose?

    A. ___You want to spend your time to teach him numbers and help him remember his "ABCs" instead of just playing with him.

    B. ___You play what he wants to play with him, because that shows you are accepting him and helping him establish confidence and autonomy.

C. ___You can be creative in including the numbers or alphabet in the playtime, and keep his interest while playing with him.

9. Your friends have different opinions regarding communication with school-age children. Which one is your belief? Explain why.

A. ___Children should be encouraged to express their feelings and thoughts at any time.

B. ___Training children to refrain from expressing their feelings helps them be patient and endure pain.

C. ___Parents should allow and encourage children to express themselves when the situation is appropriate.

10. Adolescence is a difficult stage for both parents and children. Some effective ways to communicate with an adolescent are to:

A. ___Avoid conflict by ignoring him/her.

B. ___Use "I" messages to communicate.

C. ___Use "you" messages to communicate.

D. ___ Listen with an open minded-attitude.

E. ___ Model respect and trust in your communication.

11. Billy is 17 years old. He is making a decision about college applications. His parents want him to go to the same university as his sister, so his sister can take care of him. Billy tells his parents that he wants to be independent, and that his sister is too controlling. Which suggestion would you give to Billy's mother?

A. ___ Parents have the right to make decisions for their children, so they should insist that Billy apply to his sister's school.

B. ___ Tell Billy that if he goes to the same school, they will buy a new car for him.

C. ___ Tell Billy that college is for study, not "to be independent."

D. ___ Billy's parents need to talk with Billy and understand his feelings and thoughts about going to college.

12. Ted, a 13-year-old boy, returned from his friend Donny's

house, and told his mother, "See, Mom, Donny's mom allows Donny (who is the same age as Ted) to have girlfriends." If Ted's mother asks your advice, which suggestion(s) would you give to her?

A. ___Ignore Ted. All the adolescent boys are interested in girls.

B. ___Don't let Ted associate with Donny because Donny is a bad influence.

C. ___Be patient with adolescents, and have an open-minded discussion with Ted.

13. Jan, a high school senior, was having dinner with her parents. Jan's mother started to talk about her friend's daughter, Mary. She said, "You know Mary is going to hold a graduation recital soon, and her mother told me Mary has received a music scholarship. They are lucky!" Jan was quiet, but soon she picked up her plate and left. She went to her room and closed the door. Why did Jan leave the dinner table?

A. ___Because of Jan's poor social skills.

B. ___Because Mary's success made Jan look bad.

C. ___Because of her mother's negative comparison.

14. Which of the following would be your suggestion to Jan's mother?

A. ___Knock on Jan's door and apologize to her, and try to comfort her.

B. ___Knock on Jan's door and tell her that her attitude at dinner was not acceptable.

C. ___Tell Jan's father to go talk to Jan.

D. ___Just ignore her—tomorrow is another day for her.

15. A man tells his therapist that he has loved his wife since the first time he saw her. Now he is wondering, "Why is my wife unhappy with me?" He says, "My therapist has told me, 'you both need to improve your communication.' I don't understand!" What is your opinion about this husband's comment?

A. ___The husband still loves his wife, but his wife may need to share her feelings and thoughts more often. Couple's communication should go both ways.

B. ___The wife may not have felt her husband's love, so he should put more effort into expressing his love.

16. Cultural differences between a couple can provide wonderful learning experiences, yet may create chaotic misunderstandings for the couple. What is your suggestion?

A. ___One partner or spouse needs to be submissive and follow the other partner.

B. ___The couple needs to have an open-minded attitude and be willing to listen and share.

C. ___The couple may ignore cultural differences, because the love between them is more important.

17. Effective communication builds trust in the relationship. Which of the following is helpful in building trust in the relationship?

A. ___Proper self-disclosure.

B. ___Listening but not talking.

C. ___Sweet talk.

18. Conflict is an inevitable issue in human relationships. From the following, which one is your recommendation for resolving conflict?

    A. ___ For the sake of peace, just apologize!

    B. ___ Fight for your own rights. Don't just give in.

    C. ___ Bring out the conflict issue, listen to each other's point(s) and be fair to each other.

19. Mrs. Brown is visiting her adult son, Marc, who is married and has a 4-year-old boy, Jimmy. At 8 o'clock, Jimmy was supposed to take a bath and go to bed, but Jimmy would not follow his mother's instructions. He wanted to continue playing with the new toy that his grandma bought him. Jimmy's mother, Beth, was very upset and loudly yelled at Jimmy. Jimmy cried, and everybody was in a bad mood. Then Grandma stepped in to rescue Jimmy and said, "It's all right. He may skip his bath today. He did not sweat, and he was a good boy today." What would you think about Mrs. Brown's comment?

    A. ___ It creates a "triangulation."

    B. ___ It provides a peaceful instruction.

    C. ___ Grandma was a helpful rescuer to her grandson.

20. In the above situation, Marc (Mrs. Brown's son) appeared to be uneasy. What is your suggestion for Marc?

    A. ___He should talk to his mother nicely: "Mom, the 8 o'clock bath is both Beth's and my decision, and it's a routine Jimmy needs to follow." Then he should help Jimmy take his bath.

    B. ___He should avoid involvement by withdrawing to his study.

    C. ___He should show support to his wife by punishing Jimmy with a 5-minute time-out.

    D. ___He should tell his mother, "Mom, don't spoil your grandkid!"

21. While her daughter was out, Mrs. Block took a telephone message for her, but she purposely did not give the message to her daughter, because she did not like the caller, a friend her daughter was associating with.

    A. ___Mrs. Block did the right thing, because she believes that friend is a bad influence.

    B. ___Mrs. Block should not withhold the message,

but she can discuss her concerns with her daughter at an appropriate time.

C. ___Mrs. Block should just give the message to her daughter regardless of her own concern.

22. Children in blended families need to adjust to their new parents and siblings. The parents need to be able to communicate effectively. Which of the following do you think would be your choice(s)?

A. ___Minimizing communication in order to avoid conflict.

B. ___Communicating with direct and clear messages in order to avoid entanglement.

C. ___Being open-minded and embodying positive attitudes to help the children's communication.

23. Last Christmas was the first holiday together for Lori and Stan. They decided to invite the relatives who live nearby to join their Christmas dinner. After dinner, the conversations were centered on current information about relatives. One of the cousins was in trouble with substance abuse and had been sentenced to jail. Lori

was relatively new in the family and she felt that their discussion was just gossip. What is your suggestion for Lori?

    A. ___Just get away from the discussion.

    B. ___Since Lori is the hostess; she should initiate a new situation, like suggesting they play a game, or dance.

    C. ___Condemn their behavior and stop them from gossiping.

24. The communication in a blended family is not always easy because family members have different experiences and different communication patterns. When June and Ben remarry, they both will have children from previous marriages. From the following list, what would you suggest to June and Ben, so they may have a happy blended family?

    A. ___June and Ben need to take time to know each other better, and to take time preparing their children for their remarriage.

    B. ___June and Ben need to be open-minded,

able to listen and able to express their own feelings and thoughts.

C. ___They should avoid taking sides with their own children in order to be fair to all the children.

D. ___They should set rules that all the members can follow.

E. ___They should support open communication.

F. ___All the above.

THE ANSWERS TO THE TESTS

1. C.

2. Use your own discretion.

3. Depends on the answer to #2.

4. A.

5. B

6. B

7. A

8. C.

9. C.

10. B, D, E.

11. D.

12. C

13. C.

14. A.

15. A.

16. B.

17. A

18. C.

19. A.

20. A.

21. B.

22. B, C.

23. B.

24. F.

References

Berne, E. (1961). *Transactional Analysis in Psychotherapy.* New York: Grove Press, Press, P 24

Bowen, M. (1978) *Family therapy in clinical Practice.* New York, Jason Aronson, Inc.

Erikson, E.H. (1959). *Identity and the life Cycle,* New York: International University Press, PP 88- 90

Hoffman, L. (1981) *Foundations of Family Therapy.* New York, Basic Books, Inc.

Mckay, M., Davis, M. & Fanning, P. (1995) *Messages.* Second Edition Oakland, CA. New Harbinger Publications, Inc.

Nichols, W. (1988) *Marital Therapy.* New York, Guilford Press.

Sharpe, S. (2000) *The Way We Love.* New York, Guilford Press.

Tannen, D. (1990) *You Just Don't Understand.* New York, Ballantine Books.

Printed in the United States
77929LV00006B/1-9

9 781432 700843